Real Wales

A Guide by Heini Gruffudd

First impression: 1998
Reprinted: 2001
© 1998 Y Lolfa Cyf. and Heini Gruffudd

Book and cover design: Owain Huw

Photographs: Heini Gruffudd unless otherwise stated

Thanks to The National Library of Wales, Cymdeithas yr Iaith,
S4C, Marian Delyth, Keith Morris and Emlyn Phillips for the
use of their photographs

ISBN: 0 86243 423 8

Printed and published in Wales by:
Y Lolfa Cyf., Talybont, Ceredigion, SY24 5AP
✉ylolfa@ylolfa.com ▢http://www.ylolfa.com
☎+44 (0)1970 832 304 ▤832 782

Real Wales

A Guide by Heini Gruffudd

I Rob
am ei gyfraniad
i'r traddodiad

contents

wales – an introduction 7

wales – the nation 9

highlights and lowlights of welsh history: 15

    pre-history 16

    early history 19

    age of saints 23

    age of welsh kings and princes 25

    wales in the middle ages 39

    early modern wales 45

    recent history 50

customs 84

tales 87

government in wales 91

popular culture 93

the future for wales 94

a taste of welsh 95

information contacts 110

further reading 112

wales – an introduction

The purpose of this book is to give an easy introduction to the story of Wales. To understand what Wales means to Welsh people, one must have an idea about the country's history. This includes the origins of Wales, the age of Welsh kings and princes, the story of the Welsh language and, more recently, the struggle for a national identity and the efforts to safeguard the language.

That a small nation such as Wales has survived in the shadow of one of the world's greatest powers must be one of the most remarkable stories of western society.

Although Wales has not ruled itself for more than five hundred years, its language is still alive, and its sense of identity is strong. As such, it is the envy of many other of Europe's smaller countries which are in danger of losing their language and identity. Welsh medium education is flourishing, as is its radio and television service. The number of people speaking Welsh is rising.

A hundred years or so ago, Wales had only a handful of national institutions. Today it is served by more than a hundred national bodies, movements and institutions, and is developing its own system of government once again. Special attention is paid to this remarkable turnaround.

All this action is played against the background of the beautiful Welsh countryside, shown in the numerous pictures.

All of this should hopefully whet the appetite of those who live in Wales and visitors to the country who wish to know more about the remarkable survival of Wales.

HEINI GRUFFUDD

The British Isles

Wales

wales – the nation

National Boundaries

The boundary between Wales and England has been fairly constant for the last one and a half thousand years. When the English King Offa built his dyke to separate his kingdom from the Welsh around the year 750 he acknowledged an existing boundary that has remained roughly the same until today. This dyke is around 150 miles long, and much of it can be walked along today.

As with almost all countries, the territorial claims have varied. At one time parts of Herefordshire and Gloucestershire were ruled by Welsh princes. A large number of Welsh people have lived in towns and cities on the English side of the border, such as Hereford and Liverpool. In turn, Flemish people settled in southern Pembrokeshire, and Normans settled in towns around their Welsh castles. In the last hundred years large numbers of English people have come to live in Wales, particularly along the south-east and north-east coast. There was a dispute at one time over the south-eastern county of Monmouth, or Gwent. Nevertheless, the distinct border between Wales and England has by now been acknowledged by the parliament in London.

Previous Lands of the Welsh

The idea that the Welsh have only lived in Wales is however erroneous. The first Welsh poetry was written in southern Scotland and northern England.

Many places in England derive from Welsh or Celtic names, e.g. Dover (*dwfr* = water), Lincoln (*llyn* = lake). Before the Angles and the Saxons came to invade Britain from the continent, the land was generally inhabited by people who spoke an old form of Welsh. This language had in turn developed from a Britannic language, which belonged to the Celtic languages. The oldest Wales, therefore, could be said to be most of the island of Britain. The first Welsh poems which we know about were written in northern England or southern Scotland in the 6th century, and a Welsh poem of the

The Welsh Language

The main language of Wales, from the beginnings of Wales until 1900, was Welsh. The language is derived from the Celtic group of languages. This in turn belongs to the main group of languages which spread across Europe and Western Asia, sometimes called Indo-European. The Celtic group has six different languages, split into two sub-groups: Irish (spoken in Ireland), Gaelic (Scotland) and Manx (Isle of Man) belong closely together, while Cornish (Cornwall), Breton (Brittany) and Welsh belong to the other group. Of these languages, Welsh is the most flourishing today.

How many speak Welsh?

Welsh is spoken by around half a million people in Wales (census statistics, 1991), but perhaps another quarter of a million people can speak some Welsh, and many more can understand the language. Around 20% of the people of Wales speak it. The constant decline of the language during the 20th century, which began with around 50% of the population of Wales speaking Welsh, has at last been halted. The actual number of people speaking Welsh in Wales has fallen from nearly

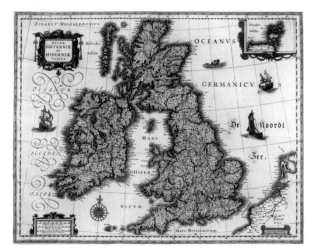

One of the first printed maps of Wales, published in an Atlas of England and Wales by Christopher Sexton in the 16th century

9th century, *Armes Prydein* (the Prophecy of Britain), looks forward to the day when the Welsh will be joined by forces from Scotland, Ireland, Cornwall and Brittany to send the English back across the sea.

Numbers of Welsh speakers in Wales 1891–1991

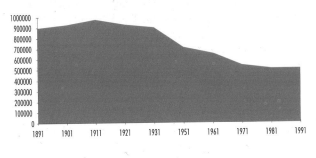

Percentage of Welsh speakers in Wales 1891–1991

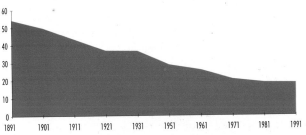

a million to half a million, and it has steadied at around this figure. The percentage of Welsh speakers has also steadied, at just below 20%.

Huge immigration into Wales at the turn of the century, the two world wars and the years of economic depression between the wars, when around half a million people left Wales, have had a detrimental effect on the fate of the Welsh language. But at long last it is slowly recovering.

While the number of old people speaking Welsh has been declining, the numbers of young people speaking the language is increasing dramatically. This is due to the success of the Welsh medium schools which are to be found in all parts of Wales. Many non-Welsh speakers send their children there to learn Welsh (and English of course) because they themselves did not have the opportunity to do so. In many such schools in south-east Wales, around 90% of the children come from English speaking homes. Around 25% of school pupils in Wales attend Welsh medium schools, and it is the education policy in many parts of north and west Wales that all children become bilingual. Pupils in English medium schools throughout Wales now learn Welsh as a second language.

Welsh speakers, 1991

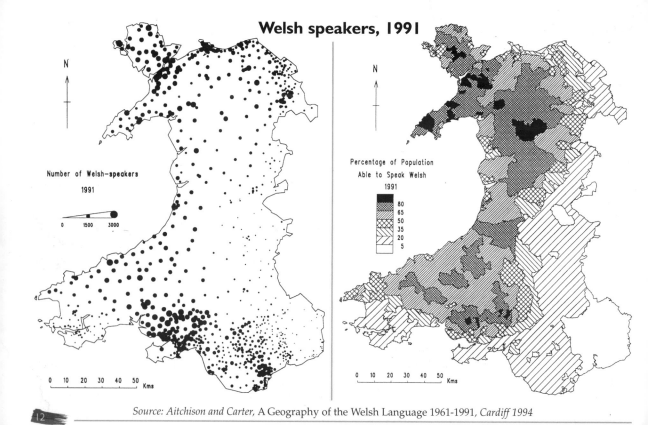

N

Number of Welsh-speakers
1991

0   1500   3000

0 10 20 30 40 50 Kms

N

Percentage of Population
Able to Speak Welsh
1991

80
65
50
35
20
5

0 10 20 30 40 50 Kms

Source: Aitchison and Carter, A Geography of the Welsh Language 1961-1991, *Cardiff 1994*

Where is Welsh Spoken?

Welsh is spoken all over Wales. Some areas, particularly in north and west Wales, are regarded as Welsh-speaking Wales because the percentage of Welsh speakers there is over 50%. Some areas still have more than 70% Welsh speakers, although many rural areas have suffered because of the effects of tourism, second homes, and immigration from England. Nevertheless, towns such as Caernarfon in North Wales, and Cardigan and Carmarthen in South Wales, are still very Welsh speaking. But for actual numbers, the area where most Welsh is spoken is in south and south-west Wales, around the towns of Carmarthen, Llanelli, Ammanford and Swansea. Welsh is more used as a language of commerce and of society at large, e.g. in shops and pubs, in areas of north and west Wales.

Very little Welsh is spoken in this Cardiff pub but the feeling of Welshness is still strong

What makes Wales Welsh?

Different people would give you different answers. No one, however, will deny that most Welsh people regard themselves as Welsh and not English, and most would regard themselves as Welsh and not British, or Welsh first, at any rate. People regard themselves as Welsh because they belong to the nation of Wales. They belong either because they live in Wales, or because their ancestors lived in Wales. They belong to a people who have inhabited the same piece of land for two thousand years. They have spoken a distinct language for most of that time. They have shared a common history, and they share common economic and cultural experiences. Sometimes they share common political aspirations.

Many would argue that Welsh people are egalitarian and socialist. Others would say they are literate and religious. You often hear that Welsh people like singing and talking. Some would say that Welsh people lack political guts and are prone to seeking favours from the English instead of uniting and acting independently. On the other hand, Welsh people are often anti-authoritarian and humorous. All this tends to make Welsh people argue as to what being Welsh means to them.

highlights and lowlights
of welsh history

The Iberians

If you look around you in Wales, you will find that many people are fairly short, and many are dark haired. These characteristics were probably not inherited from the Celts. They are more likely to be inherited from an Iberian (Spanish peninsula) people who could have crossed the seas long before the Celts, probably from 2,000 BC onwards. They are associated with the *cromlechs* (groups of large standing stones on which a large boulder is balanced) and with Stonehenge, other stone circles and with individual standing stones. The *cromlechs*, whose stones are today exposed, were at one time covered by soil and used as burial chambers, but there is still some argument as to the use of the larger stone circles. They could have been used as temples, but they were certainly not originally connected with the Druids, who were political and religious leaders of the later Celtic Welsh society. Many bronze and gold objects in Wales and Ireland belong to this period.

The stones used to build Stonehenge were taken from the Preseli hills in Pembrokeshire, south-west Wales, and were probably carried by boat from Milford Haven across the sea and then up river. The enormity of this task should not be underestimated even though stone age people were master technicians and sailors.

The Cromlech at Pentre Ifan, Pembrokeshire, was built in the pre-Celtic era. Stones from the nearby Preseli hills were removed to build Stonhenge in Southern England.

The Celts

The early Welsh inherited their language and culture from the Celts, who around 600-100 BC dominated or inhabited large parts of Europe. They even captured Rome in 390 BC. From their original lands in the Austrian region they spread to large parts of Eastern and Western Europe, including parts of Turkey in the east, and France and Spain in the west, but they in turn were defeated by the rise of Rome from around 250 BC onwards. The Celts crossed to Britain, and then to Wales, in the years following or around 500 BC. Many hill forts in Wales and on the continent belong to this period, and the Celts are generally associated with the Bronze Age and Iron Age. The Celts introduced iron implements and were well equipped to deal with many kinds of metals, as is shown particularly by a hoard found in a lake in Anglesey – Llyn Cerrig Bach. Many beautifully designed Celtic objects can be seen today in the National Museum of Wales in Cardiff and in the British Museum in London. The weapons, jewellery and other objects which have been found from this period show that the Celts had highly developed skills in art and metalwork, and the intricate spirals and stone work on brooches, shields and swords reveal a standard of craftsmanship that has not been surpassed.

The Celts had their own religious system, which included a large number of gods, often associated with natural phenomena, such as rivers, lakes, trees and animals, many of whom are converted into mythological characters in Welsh and Irish mediaeval tales. Early Welsh tales, written around the 12th century but which date back to earlier times, have been collected under the general title *Mabinogi* or *Mabinogion*, meaning 'tales of youth'. Examples of Celtic gods in the Welsh Mabinogi tales include Gofannon, a divine smith, Mabon, the divine youth, and Modron, the divine mother. Another is Lleu,

who is associated with the Irish Lugh, who corresponds to the Roman god Mercury, and the god Lugus whose name is still commemorated in the French town of Lyon. Association with animals is seen in the persons of Rhiannon, associated with the Celtic horse goddess Epona, and Owain, associated with Cernunnos the lord of animals, whose horn-headed figure appears on the Gundestrup cauldron.

The Celtic religious system in Wales was led by the Druids, who were probably political leaders as well.

Carew Cross, Pembrokeshire – a Celtic cross from the 9th century

The Romans Came, Conquered and Left...

Many historians think of Wales as having begun its independent history around the time the Romans left Wales. This also happens to be the time the Welsh language developed out of the previous Britannic language and it also leads up to the time the borders of present day Wales became more or less settled. Moreover it is also the time when Christianity became the religion of Wales. Julius Caesar had landed in Britain around 55 BC, but the main attacks on Wales happened between 40 and 80 AD, when around 30,000 Roman soldiers were involved in the fighting against the tenacious Welsh tribes, especially against the Silures of South Wales. Julius Frontinus led a successful campaign against the latter, and set up the fortress at Caerleon around 75 AD. Agricola led the Roman conquest of North Wales, and established the Roman fort at Segontium (Caernarfon). The last Roman ruler was Magnus Maximus, or Macsen Wledig, and he left Wales around 383 AD with ambitions to become the Roman emperor.

The Romans left behind them a network of good roads, towns and forts, and metal industries. They had established large forts at Deva (Chester), Isca

The Roman amphitheatre at Caerleon, Gwent, where the Romans had a substantial fort and town

(Caerleon), Segontium (Caernarfon) and Maridunum (Carmarthen), and had linked these and other centres with efficient roads. They had mined gold at Dolau Cothi in Carmarthenshire, South Wales and copper on Parys Mountain in Anglesey.

The sparse descriptions that we have of Welsh life in this period come mainly from Latin authors, such as Tacitus, who gives a colourful description of the Roman attack on Anglesey, and of the way the Druids were killed. Welsh, or Celtic, defenders of Wales and Britain include Buddug (*Boudicca*) and Caradog (*Caratacus*).

The Welsh tribes in Wales at that time were the Venedotae in north-west Wales (corresponding to the name 'Gwynedd'), the Deceangli in north-east Wales, the Ordovices in mid-Wales, the Demetae in south-west Wales and the Silures in the south-east.

As the years went by, it seems that the Welsh and Romans coexisted more peacefully, allowing for a mixture of cultures, religion and language. Roman towns, including baths, set a new standard of civilisation; Latin and Britannic were the languages of bilingual towns, and many Latin words were borrowed by the Britannic language, which developed into Welsh. Some words borrowed into Welsh came from the Roman way of living and fighting, e.g. caer (*fort*), pont (*bridge*), llyfr (*book*), ffenestr (*window*) and ystafell (*room*). Borrowings of common words, such as pysgodyn (*fish*, from 'piscis') and braich (*arm*, from 'bracchium'), caws (*cheese*), coes (*leg*), coch (*red*), cwmwl (*cloud*), anifail (*animal*) and ffrwyth (*fruit*) suggest the bilingual nature of the society.

Defence against the Anglo Saxons

After the departure of the Romans, the Welsh had their own rulers, and it is presumed that the early political and military leaders had been entrusted by the Romans to defend their various territories. During the next few hundred years, one of their main tasks was to defend Britain against the invading Angles and Saxons, which they accomplished sometimes with success, but with ultimate defeat in parts of the country to the east of present day Wales.

The Irish also invaded Wales from the west and settled in many parts of the country. In an attempt to defend the country against the Irish, according to the Latin history of Britain, *Historia Brittonum* attributed to Nennius, a military leader from southern Scotland, Cunedda Wledig (Gwledig = Leader), was called to

Wales around 400 AD, and many parts of Wales are still named after some of his eight sons and grandsons (*see page 25*).

The first recorded experience of the early battles against the Saxons is found in an early Welsh 1,480 line epic poem, *Y Gododdin*, (the name of a Welsh kingdom and tribe in southern Scotland) written by Aneirin around 600, which describes a band of 300 Welsh warriors preparing themselves for battle against the English at Catterick, in northern England. Only three returned alive, although the defeated had fought heroically. These are lines from the poem, which was possibly written in a Welsh-Cumbrian dialect, but which can be fairly well understood today:

Gwŷr a aeth Gatraeth oedd ffraeth eu llu;
Glasfedd eu hancwyn, a gwenwyn fu.
Trichant trwy beiriant yn catau –
A gwedi elwch tawelwch fu.

The men who went to Catterick were a lively band;
New mead was their drink, and it became their poison.
Three hundred battling under command –
And after the tumult there was silence.

In this poem Aneirin celebrates the fallen Welsh warriors who were beaten in battle.

The most famous of the defenders of Wales was Arthur, but very little is known about him. He may have fought mainly in northern England or in the south-west, but he is regarded as a very successful military leader. Many years after his death, accounts were written of his famous victory at Mount Badon which could have been in the area of Bath, around 500 AD. Whatever the historical truth, his name flourished, and in an age which could easily mix history, religion

Arthur's stone, Gower, one of many geographical features connected to the historic and legendary Arthur

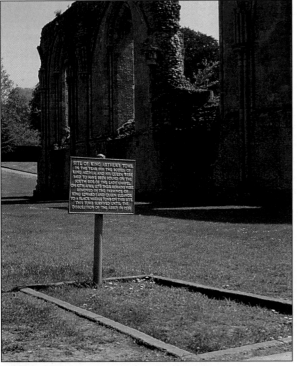

The site of Arthur's supposed grave at Glastonbury abbey

and legend, his name became associated with many parts of Wales and England.

Three early Welsh mediaeval tales refer to Arthur, as do some early Welsh poems. The Norman-Breton Welshman, Geoffrey of Monmouth, wrote a history of Britain in the twelfth century, and gave a prominent place to Arthur as an early Welsh military leader. Later romantic French tales, originally possibly of Irish and Welsh origin, were associated with him, and he became a European figure, connected with a court of knights and the search for the holy grail. Poems have been written on Arthurian themes in recent times by Tennyson in England and T.Gwynn Jones in Wales in the twentieth century.

Giraldus Cambrensis, or Gerald of Wales, Wales' greatest Latin writer, (born 1146 at Manorbier, Pembrokeshire, of Welsh and Norman descent) wrote books about many places in England, Wales and Ireland in the twelfth century, and he describes how the monks at Glastonbury claimed to have discovered the grave of Arthur and his wife Gwenhwyfar (*Guinevere*).

age of saints

After the Romans left Wales, monks spread Christianity throughout Wales and other Celtic countries. The sixth and seventh centuries are known as the Age of Saints. It was during this time that monks, or religious leaders, such as Padarn, Teilo and Illtud, Dyfrig and Cadog set up churches and establishments of learning, many of which are still named after them. The leading monks became bishops of their churches, such as Bishop Padarn whose centre was at Llanbadarn Fawr, near Aberystwyth. Three main churches had developed by the time of the Norman invasion, at Bangor, Llandaff and St. Davids, but one of the most important educational establishments was at Llanilltud Fawr (Llantwit Major) in Glamorgan.

The cathedral at St. Davids, Pembrokeshire

There are more than 400 place names in Wales today which begin with the word 'Llan', which means 'church', and it is often followed by the name of one of these monks, e.g. Llandeilo = the church of Teilo; Llanilltud = the church of Illtud; Llangadog = the church of Cadog. The most well known of these monks, or saints, is Dewi, or David, and he became the patron saint of Wales, whose day is celebrated on March 1. The number of churches attributed to him in Wales and other parts of the country suggests that he travelled

Ynys Enlli (Bardsey Island), reputed to be the resting place of 20,000 saints

widely. Several churches in Wales and Cornwall are also dedicated to his mother Non. Dewi died, it is said, in 589, but his history was not written until the 11th century by a certain Rhygyfarch, whose Latin manuscript is kept at Trinity College, Dublin. The latter's main concern seems to have been to establish the independence of the Welsh church in the face of Norman influence. The stories associated with St David include his miraculous cure from blindness of his teacher, Paulinus, and the raising of the ground when he preached a sermon at Llanddewibrefi in south-west Wales. It is also claimed that he went with Teilo and Padarn on a pilgrimage to Jerusalem, where he was consecrated as an archbishop. David is supposedly buried in St David's cathedral (Tyddewi) in Pembrokeshire, and in medieval times, three pilgrimages to St David's were considered to be worth two to Rome and one pilgrimage to Jerusalem.

age of welsh kings and princes

For about nine hundred years after the Romans left Wales, the country was ruled by its own kings who were heads of several royal houses. The sense of unity in Wales would depend more on the territory inhabited by the Welsh, and by the territory in which Welsh was spoken, than by a common ruler. There were at times rulers of parts of the country, and at other times a ruler would succeed in uniting the whole country. The next centuries in Welsh history saw the development of several Welsh kingdoms; the north-western kingdom of Gwynedd eventually became the strongest, but others, such as Powys (mid and north-east Wales) and Deheubarth (south-west Wales) maintained their independence for several centuries.

Although at times they fought amongst themselves for domination in their own territory, they found common enemies in the invaders who tried to take over parts of the country. These included the Angles, Saxons, Irish, Danes, Vikings and Normans. From an early period some Welsh kings tried to form an alliance with the English invaders in order to strengthen their position, but the Welsh kings and princes retained their independence until the defeat of Llywelyn II at the hands of the Norman English in 1282.

Cunedda

It is said that a Welsh ruler, Cunedda, came to Wales in the 5th century AD from north of England and southern Scotland in order to defend Wales from the invading Irish. He divided large parts of north-west Wales between his eight sons and grandson. These areas are still named after these sons, e.g. Ceredigion (after Ceredig), Edeyrnion in Clwyd (Edern) and Meironydd (Meirion, his grandson). Nevertheless, one must view with a certain amount of scepticism the writings of Nennius, of around 800 AD, and parts of this history could simply be an attempt to explain place names.

Maelgwn Gwynedd

One of the earliest Welsh kings who succeeded in strengthening the kingdom of Gwynedd was Maelgwn Gwynedd who is said to have been a great-grandson of Cunedda. According to tradition he became king after defeating his rivals in a competition to withstand the tide, by using a chair which floated. He was condemned by religious writers of his day for murdering his wife and nephew, and then marrying his nephew's widow. This criticism, however, might have been an account by people who were unwilling to see the church's power replaced by a military ruler. Others write of his repentance, and of his might as a ruler. He died in 547 of the yellow plague.

Cadwallon

Cadwallon, who died in 633, was king of Gwynedd and the only Welsh king to have defeated the English rulers. Cadwallon linked forces with Penda, the king of Mercia, and killed Edwin the English ruler in a battle near Doncaster in 632. This raised the hopes of the Welsh of regaining the land of England, but in the following year, Cadwallon, having killed two of Edwin's successors, was killed in battle by the forces of another English successor, Oswald.

Cadwaladr

Cadwaladr, who died in 664 was the son of Cadwallon, king of Gwynedd. It is with Cadwaladr that the history manuscript, *Brut y Tywysogyon* (Chronicle of the Princes) starts. He and Cynan are often seen as the leaders who will return to Wales in its hour of need to save the Welsh from the English foe. Henry VII claimed that he was a descendant of Cadwaladr, and he flew the Red Dragon at the battle of Bosworth in 1485 in the belief that it was Cadwaladr's flag.

Rhodri Mawr

It has been suggested that Rhodri Mawr (Rhodri the Great) was the greatest of all Welsh kings. He became king of Gwynedd in 844 and king of Powys in 855. At a time when the English were pressing hard on Welsh lands, he succeeded in uniting Gwynedd, Powys and Seisyllwg (mid south-west Wales). He also resisted the onslaught on the eastern boundary and the attacks of the Danes on Anglesey, where Horm, the Danish leader, was killed. Rhodri was killed in a battle in 877, but he had established a pattern of defending the country against foreign invaders. His grandson, Hywel Dda (see below) was instrumental in compiling the Welsh Laws.

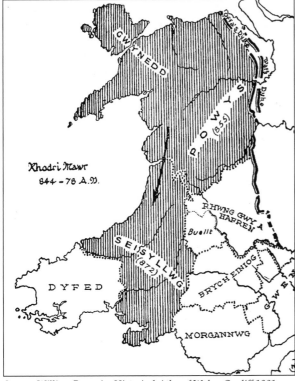

Source: William Rees, An Historical Atlas of Wales, Cardiff 1981

Welsh Education

During these centuries a varied and rich pattern of education developed in Wales. The early centres of education were connected with the church and with the courts. The early Welsh churches, which were also in some places centres of education, provided education in religious matters and probably in languages, as Welsh and Latin were used. One of the most important was at Llanilltud Fawr (*Llantwit Major*). By the end of the age of the Welsh princes, an educated person would be fluent in Welsh, Latin, French and English.

At the same time a system of education was developed by the Welsh poets, who were important officers of the kings' courts. They were the keepers of linealogy and they were also the guardians of historical events; they recorded battles and sang the praises of the kings and princes, especially their bravery in battle and their generosity at court. They also developed a highly intricate form of poetry writing, involving repetition of consonants and rhymes ('cynghanedd' in Welsh), which has lasted until today.

The first recorded national bardic and music competition ('eisteddfod') was held at the court of Rhys ap Gruffudd at Cardigan in 1176.

The Mabinogion

Another form of education was provided by the story tellers, who would entertain the courts. These memorised tales of rich imagination, which combined historic events, pre-Christian deities, romance and supernatural creatures and happenings. Some of these have survived as the tales of the *Mabinogion*.

The first four tales relate the story of Pryderi, from his birth to his death, but many other stories are intertwined.

These include the story of Branwen, who became wife of the Irish king, Matholwch. Her jealous half-brother maimed Matholwch's horses, and when the Irish heard of this, Branwen was made a slave in the kitchen and was beaten daily. Eager for revenge, her giant brother, Bendigeidfran, led a Welsh force to Ireland, and a war ensued which destroyed the islands of Britain and Ireland.

Another story involves Blodeuwedd (*Flower Face*), a girl created from flowers. Lleu (a figure associated with Celtic divinity) was destined by his mother, Arianrhod (*Silver Circle*) not to be named, not to bear arms, and not to have a human wife. Gwydion, Arianrhod's brother, and possibly father of Lleu, contrived to give him a name and weapons, and he and Math, both magicians, formed a girl, Blodeuwedd, from flowers. After the marriage of Lleu and Blodeuwedd, she was attracted to Gronw Pebr, and together they planned to kill Lleu, who turned into an eagle on being pierced by a specially prepared spear. Gwydion restored Lleu to life, and caused Blodeuwedd to change into an owl.

The *Mabinogion* contain the first native stories about Arthur. One story, Culhwch ac Olwen, describes Culhwch's successful attempt to win Olwen as a wife. Her father, a giant, insists that Culhwch must accomplish forty impossible feats. He succeeds with the help of Arthur's knights. Other stories about Arthur, referred to in other tales, are certainly lost. Three later tales, related to the French romances, also refer to Arthur.

Another story, the Dream of Macsen, portrays Macsen Wledig, Magnus Maximus of history, dreaming about a girl in Caernarfon. He sets out from Rome to find her, and succeeds. Later he is made emperor of Rome with the help of Welsh warriors.

Welsh Laws

During the reign of Hywel Dda (Hywel the Good) it is evident that Wales had a highly developed system of government. He is credited with assembling the Welsh laws, still called the Laws of Hywel. It is said that he held a large conference at Hendygwyn-ar-daf (*Whitland*), but the earliest copies of Welsh laws, written in Welsh and Latin, belong to the twelfth century. The laws, which were among the most advanced in Europe at that time, were administered in courts throughout the country. They continued to operate after the military conquest of Wales in 1282, and were still in force in some courts until the middle of the 16th century.

Twenty-four manuscripts of the laws remain, and they show how the laws progressively changed during the course of the centuries. The laws list the court officers, and deal with the various rules and arrangements of law. The price of a murdered man's life would have to be paid by his family to the seventh, and sometimes ninth, relative. This reflects the importance of the extended family in Welsh life, and the role of uncles in the upbringing of children. The just nature of Welsh law, which divided a father's estate

A display of early Welsh laws in the Hywel Dda commemorative gardens, Hendygwyn-ar-daf (Whitland), Carmarthenshire

equally between sons (unlike English law where the eldest son inherited all) also unfortunately divided the land at the time of the ruler's death. This caused a continual weakening in the strength of Welsh rulers, compared to their English neighbours.

Hywel Dda had, by 942, united the whole of Wales, (except for the south-east) under his crown, without resorting to battle. His diplomacy is seen by the way he acknowledged the English kings rather than warring against them, and in so doing he kept Wales at peace. Money bearing his name was minted. He was the only Welsh king to have accomplished this.

Maredudd ap Owain and Gruffudd ap Llywelyn

During the period following Hywel Dda's death in 950, Wales was attacked continually by the English and the Danes. Most of Wales was once again united under the reign of Maredudd ap Owain ('ap' means 'son of'), Hywel Dda's grandson, who ruled from 986-999, and then by Gruffudd ap Llywelyn, who was the first to face the Norman invaders. He defeated a force of English and Normans in 1052 at Leominster. He was the only native king to succeed in uniting the whole of Wales, from 1055 to 1063, and he regained Welsh land on the eastern side of Offa's Dyke. Harold, the Earl of Wessex, led an attack on Wales, partly because of Gruffudd's interference in English affairs, and Gruffudd was eventually killed at the hands of his own men who had been bought by Harold. Gruffudd's head was sent to Harold.

There followed two centuries of fierce fighting against the Norman invaders until the Welsh were finally defeated in 1282. The Welsh had to agree to pay homage to the Norman or English kings in order to secure peace. At times marriages were arranged between the Welsh princes and daughters of the Norman king or local rulers; at other times fierce battles were fought. The English kings awarded Welsh lands to their lords in Wales so that Norman rule gradually gained ground on the border lands and in South Wales.

Churches, Abbeys and Monasteries

During this period, monasteries and abbeys were being built in many parts of Wales by orders of monks from France. St Davids, Llandaff and Bangor and then St Asaph were chosen in the twelfth century as the seats of bishops and the country was divided into dioceses and parishes. In spite of attempts to preserve a separate Welsh church, by the 12th century Canterbury was acknowledged as the head church. By collecting tithes (a tenth of the annual increase of all stock and crops in the parish, and one out of ten animals) the local rectors, priests, or monastic houses accumulated wealth, so that the bishops became large landowners.

Houses of many monastic orders were established in Wales after the Norman conquest of England. The Cistercian order was one of the main builders of abbeys, which were built with the support of both Norman and Welsh rulers. Abbeys were established by the Cistercians at Tintern (1131), Margam (1147), Neath (1139), Talley (1184-9), Whitland (1140), Cwm Hir

(1143), Strata Florida (1164, at the invitation of Gruffudd ap Rhys), Cymer (1199, with the support of Llywelyn Fawr), Aberconwy (1186, founded by Llywelyn Fawr), Valle Crucis (1201, with the support of Madog ap Gruffudd) and other places. Their ruins are still to be seen today. There were Benedictine establishments at Cardiff, Ewenny, Kidwelly, Cardigan, Llanbadarn, and Penmon in Anglesey.

The monastic orders, which were often supported by the local Welsh rulers, became large land owners, and they became part of the religious and cultural life of Wales. Many of the early Welsh manuscripts were written by monks at these monasteries.

Welsh Government

The government of Wales, at the time of the invasion of the Normans, was organised according to territories known as 'gwlad' (*country*), and 'cantref' (*hundred; hundred houses*) and 'cwmwd' (*commote*). The 'gwlad' was an area such as Gwynedd or Powys in the north and Dyfed and Brycheiniog (*Brecon*) in the south. The king's court ruled the 'gwlad' which consisted of many officers of court including the steward, judge, falconer, court priest and court bard.

The abbey at Talyllychau (Talley) near Llandeilo. This was given financial aid by Rhys ap Gruffudd (12th century) and a gravestone marks the possible spot of the grave of Dafydd ap Gwilym (d. 1370), who is probably at rest in Ystrad Fflur (Strata Florida) abbey!

The king had lesser court houses in each 'cantref' and 'cwmwd', and these were the centres of local government, which were responsible for holding courts and the collection of dues.

If Wales had been allowed to develop as an independent country at this time – united by a common law, literature, religion, language and territory – it could well have developed a pattern of decentralised government. As it was, each Welsh kingdom in turn produced strong leaders, and only rarely was the whole country governed by a single ruler. Eventually the administrative system of England was forced on the country in an attempt to make it an inseparable part of England. It is remarkable that Wales, having been for so long a part of one of the world's greatest powers, has retained its separate identity.

Rhys ap Tewdwr and Gruffudd ap Cynan

One of Wales' influential rulers was Rhys ap Tewdwr of Deheubarth (Cardiganshire and most of Carmarthenshire) who was killed fighting the Normans in 1093. Another was Gruffudd ap Cynan who ruled Gwynedd. He had been brought up in Dublin, and although he had been beaten in a first attempt to return to Gwynedd, and had returned to Dublin, his second attempt was more successful. With Rhys ap Tewdwr he defeated Welsh opposition in 1081, and when the Normans had made inroads after the death of Rhys ap Tewdwr in 1093, Gruffudd and his compatriots captured all the Norman castles west of Conwy. The Welsh in South Wales had similar success, capturing all the Norman castles in Ceredigion and Dyfed except for Pembroke and Rhyd-y-gors near Carmarthen.

Gwenllian and Gruffudd ap Rhys

After the death of Henry I in 1135, the Welsh took their opportunity to regain many of the lands conquered by the Normans. Gruffudd ap Rhys (the son of Rhys ap Tewdwr) went to Gwynedd to seek the help of Gruffudd ap Cynan's sons to throw the Normans out of Deheubarth. But while he was away, his wife Gwenllian (the daughter

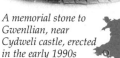

A memorial stone to Gwenllian, near Cydweli castle, erected in the early 1990s

of Gruffudd ap Cynan) fought a battle against the Norman castle and town at Cydweli (*Kidwelly*) in 1136. This followed the defeat of a Norman force at Garn Goch, Gower, in 1136 at the hands of Hywel ap Maredudd, when five hundred Normans were killed in battle. Gwenllian's army, however, was defeated by Maurice de Londres (whose grave is at Ewenny Priory).

Owain Gwynedd

Owain Gwynedd (c.1100-1170), the son of Gruffudd ap Cynan and Gwenllïan's sister, and his brother Cadwaladr joined forces with Gruffudd ap Rhys in the same year, and together they defeated a Norman force at Cardigan. Hundreds of Normans were drowned as they fled over the river. When Henry II led an expedition to Gwynedd in 1157, Owain recognised him as a feudal overlord, and relinquished the title of king for the title of prince. Nevertheless, he kept his influence over the church at Bangor, and his position as a political leader of a large part of Wales. Cadwaladr, who was ruler of Ceredigion, was removed from this post by Owain Gwynedd as he had become an ally of the Normans for a while, before rejoining his brother in their defence of Wales.

The tomb of Rhys ap Gruffudd at St David's Cathedral

Rhys ap Gruffudd

At this time, one of the greatest rulers in the south emerged. He was Rhys ap Gruffudd, the son of Gwenllian and Gruffudd ap Rhys. Rhys ap Gruffudd co-operated with Owain Gwynedd in their defence of Wales against the Norman forces. Rhys ap Gruffudd's centre was at Dinefwr (*Dynevor*) castle near Llandeilo. Following Henry II's expedition to Wales in 1157, he lost large parts of his land, but he led rebellions in 1159, 1162, and 1164 and by 1166 he had regained the former territories. It was during these campaigns that Henry II came to Pencader in 1162, and was told by the 'old man of Pencader' that it would be the Welsh who would answer for this part of Wales in the Day of Judgement, a story told by Gerald of Wales in the 12th century. This story has become a part of Welsh national consciousness. Rhys had also taken the castles of Cilgerran and Cardigan in the Teifi valley, and moved his main court from Dinefwr to Cardigan in 1171. It was at Cardigan in 1176 that he held the first eisteddfod (bardic and musical competition) that we know of, an institution that still flourishes today. He also sponsored the establishment of the abbeys at Talyllychau (*Talley*) and Ystrad Fflur (*Strata Florida*).

Dinefwr castle, Llandeilo, Carmarthenshire – the early centre of power of Rhys ap Gruffudd before his capture of Cardigan castle, 12th century

Gerallt Gymro (*Gerald of Wales*)

In 1188 Gerald of Wales, who was born at Manorbier in Pembrokeshire, went on journeys throughout Wales to gather an army for the Crusades. As was his custom, Gerald wrote about what he saw and experienced, and much of what we know about Wales in the middle ages comes from his writings. He related many folk stories, wrote of events of the day, noted conversations, described the country, and even commented on the ability of the Welsh to sing in harmony spontaneously. Among Gerald's books are *The Conquest of Ireland*, *The Topography of Ireland*, *The Journey through Wales* and *Description of Wales*. Gerald was more Norman than Welsh by blood, but he called himself Giraldus Cambrensis (i.e. Gerald of Wales). In 1198 he was nominated for the second time as Bishop of St David's, but was rejected by the Archbishop of Canterbury. Gerald then campaigned for an independent archbishopric at St David's, with himself as archbishop.

Poets of the Princes

The poets had their own orders which flourished throughout this period. The earliest known poet of the princes is Meilyr who sang an elegy to Gruffudd ap Cynan in 1137. The poets were professional writers who were important officers of court. They not only kept their own bardic traditions and supported the princes, but they were also the national conscience of the country. Some of the princes were themselves poets, and some of the finest love poetry of the period was written by Hywel ab Owain of Gwynedd. He was the brother of Madog who supposedly discovered America.

Here is part of a love poem by Hywel ab Owain:

> Fy newis i
> Fy newis i, rhiain firain feindeg,
> Hirwen, yn ei llen lliw ehöeg.
> A'm dewis synnwyr, synio ar wreigiaidd,
> Pen ddywaid o fraidd weddaidd wofeg.

> *My choice*
> *My chosen, a maid fair and slender,*
> *Tall and white, in her heather-hued gown.*
> *And my chosen lore, to watch one who's womanly,*
> *When she speaks, scarcely heard, gracious words.*

He can be equally eloquent when describing war, as in this poem to the Battle of Tâl Moelfre:

> *When crows made merry, when blood ran freely,*
> *When men's blood was poured out,*
> *When war came, when houses turned red,*
> *When shore was red, when court burned red.*

(Translations by Joseph P Clancy.)

Llywelyn Fawr (*Llywelyn the Great*)

The Normans continued in their attempts to subdue Wales, and after the death of Lord Rhys ap Gruffudd (1197), and of Owain Gwynedd, his grandfather, the onus of defending Wales lay with Llywelyn ap Iorwerth (1173-1240), of Gwynedd. His castles, such as Dolbadarn and Dolwyddelan were mostly inland, built in mountainous areas, while the Normans' castles were mainly along the coastal lowlands.

By his 24th birthday, in 1197, he was already the strongest prince in the country, but many of his early efforts were spent in defeating Gwenwynwyn of Powys, another strong leader. King John of England took advantage of this internal dispute by playing one against the other. In 1205 Llywelyn married Joan, King John's daughter, and paid homage to the king. However in 1210 John attacked Gwynedd and defeated Llywelyn, although he allowed him to retain western Gwynedd. Nevertheless, with the support of the Pope, Llywelyn fought to regain land that he lost. Following internal disputes and further struggles against the English, Llywelyn united with the English barons who opposed John. He eventually succeeded in uniting most of Wales and held a parliament of Welsh rulers near Aberdyfi in 1216. He was accepted as overlord of Welsh princes by Henry II and subsequently in 1218 by Henry III. He also succeeded in winning support for his son Dafydd as the next united leader of Wales. Llywelyn Fawr died in 1240.

Llywelyn ap Iorwerth
(Llywelyn Fawr)

Llywelyn ap Gruffudd (Llywelyn II)

Unfortunately Dafydd died in 1246 and the Normans took advantage of the opportunity to occupy large parts of Wales, both in the north and south. Llywelyn ap Gruffudd (c1225-1282), a grandson of Llywelyn Fawr, defeated his brother Owain and succeeded in winning the support of other Welsh princes, thereby adopting the title of Prince of Wales in 1258. He devoted the remainder of his career to resisting the Norman advances. By 1267 the Montgomery agreement with the English king was signed whereby Llywelyn recognised the English crown, so that he would be recognised as the Prince of Wales. Because of Llywelyn's success in winning the support of the Welshmen of northern Glamorgan, the enormous castle at Caerffili (*Caerphilly*) was built by the Normans. Unfortunately internal strife with his brother Dafydd, who united with Gruffudd ap Gwenwynwyn of Powys against Llywelyn, was followed by an attempt by Edward, the English king, to defeat Llywelyn. This led to the first war of Welsh independence, 1267-1277, which resulted in the Treaty of Aberconwy, with its harsh terms. A second war of Welsh independence was fought in 1282-83, when Llywelyn was killed at Cilmeri near Builth Wells. This event, which occurred in December 1282, possibly as a result of treachery by his own men, is still commemorated today. His body was taken to Cwmhir Abbey, twenty miles to the north, and his head was paraded around London. After a short period of resistance, his brother Dafydd was captured by the English in June 1283 and was drawn and quartered at Shrewsbury. This marked the end of the age of Welsh kings and princes.

Rhuddlan castle, north-east Wales, where the treaty of Rhuddlan was formulated

English Revenge

The revenge of the English was swift and harsh. Through the Statute of Rhuddlan, 1284, the whole country was put under the control of the king or the Norman lords, and the Welsh laws, although they could still be used in civil matters, were replaced by the English criminal law. The huge castles at Caernarfon, Conwy, Harlech, Caerffili, Pembroke and other places were built during this period. Towns were built around them where only English would be allowed to settle so that they would have a monopoly on business in these boroughs. The Welsh were made second class citizens in their own country, and as a result of this change, for years to come, the Welsh would be mainly country people, while the growing towns were mainly Norman or English.

Several attempts at rebellion were made, including one by the exiled Owain Lawgoch who raised an army of 4,000 in France to regain Wales. The poets regarded him as the prophesied saviour. He captured Guernsey from the English on his way to Wales, but was diverted to help defeat the English at La Rochelle in France. There were no longer Welsh princes who could help to unite Wales politically and militarily, but Welsh gentry, many of them direct descendants of the princes, succeeded in keeping their lands and prospered in the new peace. They continued to be patrons of the bards in a similar fashion to the princes.

Poets of the Gentry

The poets continued to write in this dark hour. While lamenting the death of Llywelyn, they still looked forward to a national leader who would lead the country to freedom. It is remarkable that it was during the 14th century, when hopes for national freedom seemed to be lost, and at a time when the country was devastated by the black plague (the Black Death), that the poets wrote some of the finest Welsh poetry ever written.

Here are a few lines of a moving elegy written by

Gruffudd ab yr Ynad Goch on the death of Llywelyn ap Gruffudd:

See you not the rush of wind and rain?
See you not the oaks lash each other?
See you not the ocean scourging the shore?
See you not the truth is portending?
See you not the sun hurtling the sky?
See you not that the stars have fallen?

. . .

Head of a soldier, head of praise,
Head of a duke, a dragon's head,
Head of fair Llywelyn, sharp the world's fear,
An iron spike through it,
Head of my lord, harsh pain is mine,
Head of my spirit left speechless. . .
Head of kings, heaven be his haven!

(Translated by Joseph P. Clancy)

The poets also experimented in the content and form of their poems. The fourteenth century poet, Dafydd ap Gwilym (fl.1320-1370) is still considered to be one of Wales' greatest poets. Unlike many other poets who had to entertain to earn their livelihood, he was one of the gentry. He wrote some of the finest love poetry written in Welsh, possibly incorporating in his verse themes that were common in the Norman-English tradition. He lived near Llanbadarn in Cardiganshire, and it is said that he is buried in the abbey at Strata Florida.

Dafydd ap Gwilym wrote much poetry about nature, and poems discussing the differences between the demands of religion and his own feelings and emotions.

The intricacies of his verse will be seen in these lines from 'Y Serch Lledrad' (*Love Kept Secret*):

Cydadrodd serch â'r ferch fain,
Cydedrych caeau didrain.
Crefft ddigerydd fydd i ferch –
Cydgerddded coed â gordderch,
Cadw wyneb, cydowenu,
Cydchwerthin finfin a fu,
Cyd-ddigwyddaw garllaw'r llwyn,
Cydochel pobl, cydachwyn,
Cydfod mwyn, cydyfed medd,
Cydarwain serch, cydorwedd,
Cyd-ddaly cariad celadwy
Cywir, ni menegir mwy.

(Together talk of love with my slim girl,
Together gaze on solitary fields.
It is a blameless occupation for a girl
To wander through the forest with her lover,
Together to keep face, together smile,
Together laugh – and it was lip to lip –
Together to lie down beside the grove,
Together to shun folk, together to complain,
To live together kindly, drinking mead together,
To rest together and express our love,
Maintaining true love in all secrecy:
There is no need to tell any more)
(Translated by Rachel Bromwich)

Dafydd ap Gwilym was the first to use 'cynghanedd' in a series of rhyming couplets, thereby creating the 'cywydd' verse form (seen above), which is still popular today.

In another poem Dafydd argues with the Grey Friar:
The Lord is not so cruel
As old men say He is.
He'll not let a dear soul go
For loving wife or maiden.
Three things are loved through the world:
Woman, health, and fair weather.

A girl's the fairest blossom
In Heaven, save God himself.
(Translated by Joseph P Clancy)

This is considered to be the golden age of Welsh poetry. Throughout the period the bards kept to a strict bardic order, organised bardic schools in which they were promoted from one grade to another, and held eisteddfodau to honour the winning poets and to establish and revise their rules.

A part of the abbey of Ystrad Fflur (Strata Florida), where a memorial stone marks the possible spot of the grave of Wales' greatest poet, Dafydd ap Gwilym

The Welsh language had also regained ground during this period particularly among the Normans who had settled in Glamorgan. Literary works from France and other European countries were translated and adapted into Welsh.

Owain Glyndŵr

In 1400 the Welsh eventually rose in rebellion. On 16th of September, after an initial local quarrel with Lord Grey of Rhuthun (*Ruthin*), Owain Glyndŵr (c.1354-c.1416), from the vale of Dee in North Wales, proclaimed himself Prince of Wales. In the following years he captured almost all the English castles in Wales, and made Harlech Castle his base. By 1401 the whole of North Wales was in revolt, with the revolt spreading to central Wales in 1402, and thereafter to the south-east. By the summer of 1403, the whole of Wales was affected, with most of it under Glyndŵr's control. He was joined by Welsh students from Oxford, and received support from all quarters of society. By 1405 all of Wales was under his rule.

One of the remarkable aspects of Glyndŵr's campaign was that he had plans for a modern and independent Welsh state. He is thus regarded by many

as the founder of modern Wales, and the father of modern Welsh nationalism. Glyndŵr formed alliances with Mortimer and Percy, Earl of Northumberland, to defeat the English king, and to divide the realm. He held a parliament at Machynlleth and at Dolgellau, after which he made a treaty with the French king. Following a parliament at Pennal (near Machynlleth) he agreed with the French king's proposal to make the Welsh Church subject to the Avignon Pope rather than the Pope at Rome. This would make St David's an archbishopric, thus making the Welsh church independent of Canterbury. Two universities, one in the north and one in the south, would also be established.

Glyndŵr began to negotiate with Robert II, king of Scotland, and with Irish rulers. He received military support from the French in the uprising of 1405, which, sadly, met with defeat. Glyndŵr's grip on the country gradually diminished, and his strongholds of Llanbadarn and Harlech were captured in 1408. By 1413 the whole country was brought into submission. Since the revolt had caused widespread destruction, the English authorities demanded compensation for loss of revenue.

Parliament house at Machynlleth, one of the sites where Owain Glyndŵr held a national Welsh parliament, early 15th century

Henry Tudor

With Owain Glyndŵr defeated, the Welsh were punished by strict laws which forbade them from holding offices under the crown, from owning property in the towns, from serving on a jury and from marrying English people. All justices, sheriffs and constables were to be English people. These laws in turn engendered a great anti-English feeling among the Welsh, whose poets continued to foresee a day when the oppression would end. Their prophecies were remarkably fulfilled when Henry Tudor (1457-1509), of part Welsh descent, won the English crown, with the help of a Welsh army, at Bosworth in 1485.

Henry Tudor was a descendant of Llywelyn Fawr. His family had been patrons of some of Wales' foremost poets and one of the family had been executed for his part in Glyndŵr's revolt. Henry, who had been born in Pembroke castle, was an exile in Brittany from 1471 to 1485 when he sailed to Wales. He defeated Richard III in the battle at Bosworth, having first collected an army of 5,000 on his march through Wales. The Welsh, who had continually desired to regain the island of Britain, thought that this had at last been achieved.

The dream that Henry was the embodiment of the

Arthur who had been longed for was short lived. Welsh nobles joined Henry VII at his court in London, and they were rewarded for their support with high offices. Unfortunately the eventual outcome of the Welsh victory at Bosworth was the anglicisation of the Welsh gentry, and the imposition of an English system of administration on Wales.

Pembroke castle, the birthplace of Henry VII, who won the English crown with the aid of a Welsh army, 1485

The Act of Incorporation and Annexation, 1536 and 1542

Under Henry VIII, the Act of Incorporation and Annexation of Wales with England (usually referred to as the Act of Union) was passed in 1536, a legislation that was completed by 1542. This act aimed to make Wales part of England administratively, and to assimilate the country linguistically and culturally. Wales was to become the first part of the forthcoming English Empire.

However, the Act gave Welsh people equality under the law, although it made English law the law of Wales. Wales was administered by thirteen counties, and was given representation in Parliament. English was to be the language of law courts and administration, and no monoglot Welsh speaker could hold any public office. Under this act Wales was to be "for ever… incorporated, united and annexed to… England" and the intention was "utterly to extirpe alle and singular the sinister usages and customs" of Wales which were different to those in England. Effectively, the administration of public life of Wales was given to those who could speak English, which was estimated to be around 5% of the population at that time.

early modern wales

The Welsh Renaissance

During the 16th century educated Welshmen were following the trends in other European countries by writing grammars and dictionaries of the Welsh language, by translating the scriptures into Welsh and by beginning to publish Welsh books, from 1546 onwards. This activity was given an impetus by the invention of the printing press, and by the Protestant Reformation.

In 1563 a law was passed to provide a Welsh translation of the Bible by March 1, 1566. The time allowed was obviously too short, but Richard Davies (1501-81), bishop of St Davids, made a valiant attempt with the aid of William Salesbury, so that their New Testament and Prayer Book were published in 1567.

The Welsh Bible was translated in full

by 1588 by Bishop William Morgan (c.1541-1604) possibly with the help of others; this translation became the basis for other versions which in turn have helped establish modern standard Welsh. The translation of the Bible was a part of the attempt to change Wales from being a Catholic country to a Protestant one, so that Wales and England would have a similar religion. Paradoxically it ensured that the Welsh language would flourish for the next three centuries. In the next 100 years 15,000 copies of the Bible were printed, about one copy for every 25 people.

The first Welsh book was published in 1547, the work of Sir John Prys. It included religious items as well as practical hints for farmers and hints on reading Welsh. In the same year William Salesbury (c.1520-c1584) published a collection of Welsh proverbs together with a Welsh-English dictionary and in 1550 the first book intended to teach Welsh.

Catholics, who had to flee the Protestant state, were also active in writing Welsh books. Gruffydd Robert (c1530-c1600) who had been educated at Oxford spent a period in Rome before settling in Milan as a church officer. He published the first Welsh grammar in 1567. By the end of the century further grammars were written by Dr Siôn Dafydd Rhys (1534-?1609), and Henry Salesbury (1561-1637). These were added to in 1621 by the famous grammar of Dr John Davies, Mallwyd (1567-1644) and in 1632 by his Welsh-Latin dictionary.

The Civil War in Wales

When the war between the English king and parliament broke out in 1642 Wales, apart from Pembroke, was mostly in favour of the king. Three main campaigns were organised. Forces from south-east Wales were involved in struggles for territories east of the border; there were several struggles in west Wales, resulting eventually in the loss of all South Wales to parliamentary forces by 1645. North Wales was mainly royalist, helped by Irish troops, but the success of the parliamentary forces at Shrewsbury turned the tide. Towns in North Wales surrendered in 1646 and 1647, many having resisted for months after the capture of Charles.

Welsh Education

By the end of the sixteenth century the native Welsh education systems, which belonged to the early church, the Welsh courts and the Welsh bards, had all but collapsed. A new system of grammar schools, which were established at Oswestry, Shrewsbury, Brecon, Abergavenny, Bangor, Carmarthen, Rhuthun and other places during the sixteenth century, gave no place to Welsh.

However, as the Welsh Bible was read in churches, a standard Welsh was being heard throughout the country. Towards the end of the seventeenth century, a 'Welsh Trust' was set up by Thomas Gouge, a London clergyman, whose aim was to teach poor children to read and write English. More than three hundred schools were established, and as Wales was largely Welsh speaking, large numbers of Welsh Bibles were distributed. This work was carried on by the Society for the Promotion of Christian Knowledge (SPCK) which distributed 10,000 copies of the Welsh Bible between 1717-18 alone.

In the eighteenth century, a system of circulating schools was established with the aim of making the Welsh people literate in their own language, and thus able to read the Bible in Welsh. The schools visited scores of Welsh villages, mostly in South Wales, for several months at a time, especially in winter when the farmers were less busy. Through the circulating schools of Griffith Jones (1683-1761) of Llanddowror, Carmarthenshire, Welsh became the medium of education for the ordinary Welsh people in the next century. During the years 1737-76, 304,475 people were taught at the schools of Griffith Jones.

These schools were followed in the nineteenth century by the Sunday schools instigated by Thomas Charles of Bala (1755-1814). In 1847 80,000 people attended these mostly Welsh medium schools, compared to 30,000 who attended daily schools, and by the middle of the nineteenth century Wales had become a land of educated people, literate in their own language.

It is no surprise that the nineteenth century was the golden age of Welsh publishing, with many papers and magazines published, as well as hundreds of other books which included Welsh novels, poetry, religious and educational books. One of the main publishers was Thomas Gee (1815-1898), who published a 10 volume, 9,000 page encyclopaedia as well as magazines and newspapers. Books on Welsh history were published in addition to a 1,100 page biographical dictionary of famous Welshmen. English and Scottish publishers joined in this profitable business and commercial travellers sold Welsh books on all subjects from house to house.

It was a body blow to the Welsh language when English was made the sole medium of compulsory education in Wales from 1870 onwards, at a time when Welsh was still the main, and indeed for many, the only language of most of the population.

Religious Revivals

After Wales had lost its Catholicism in the sixteenth century, the Church of England was the main church in Wales for the next two hundred years. Slowly, however, the nonconformist chapels gained ground, at first in the face of state opposition which involved considerable persecution. Through the hymn writing of William Williams (1717-1791), the preaching of Daniel Rowland (1713-1790) and the preaching and organisational skills of Howel Harris (1714-1773) Wales experienced a religious revival in the eighteenth century. This benefitted the nonconformist chapels greatly. At first the Methodist denomination gained most from this revival although the Baptist and Independent denominations had grown in influence from the mid seventeenth century. By 1851 87% of the population attended the nonconformist chapels, giving a seating capacity of 898,442 for a population of 1,188,914, whilst just 9% attended the Church of England. By the beginning of the twentieth century, the Welsh chapels had transformed the cultural and religious life of Wales.

William Williams

The chapels by this time were the main focus of society, being centres of Welsh cultural as well as religious life. Choirs, both mixed and male voice, were often connected with the chapels and they performed both religious and secular works. There was also a proliferation of eisteddfodau – cultural competitive events – often held in chapels, and the Gymanfa Ganu – a hymn singing festival – became a regular event, developing at first in the mining valleys of South Wales. Operettas, oratorios and plays were performed in the chapels and Wales experienced a rich cultural life due to the chapel life for a hundred years.

By 1905 the Independent denomination had 1,306 chapels, 175,147 members and 751 ministers. 162,621 attended their Sunday schools which had 15,800 teachers.

The nonconformist denominations were more Welsh than the Church of England, which often had English speaking clergy whose social links were with landlords and the English establishment. This led to a great deal of discontentment. Farmers lost their farms because they supported the growing Liberal Party instead of the Tory Party. One of the national campaigns of the nineteenth century was to disestablish the Church of England in Wales. This was finally achieved in 1920.

Early Industrialisation

Wales had been mainly a rural country although minerals had been mined in various parts of the country for two thousand years. The wool trade, with its numerous woollen mills, was important from mediaeval times onwards, and drovers used to drive cattle from Wales to be sold in English markets. Coal mining developed slowly during the Middle Ages, at Blaenafon, Caerffili, Margam, Neath and Swansea where a mine was worked at Llansamlet before 1400. Some iron, lead, copper and gold had been mined in South and North Wales.

From the sixteenth century onwards, the mining of minerals increased considerably. Iron was mined around Glamorgan, and lead in Flintshire and Cardiganshire. Coal began to be exported from Cardiff around 1600.

There were plentiful supplies of iron ore, coal, limestone and water in South Wales and these were exploited heavily towards the end of the eighteenth and beginning of the nineteenth century. The area around Merthyr Tudful (*Merthyr Tydfil*) became an important centre for producing iron and by 1811 there were 148 furnaces here.

Neath and the Swansea valley had been the main areas for producing coal, but by the middle of the 19th century the huge coal reserves in the Taf (*Taff*), Cynon and Rhondda valleys were being exploited.

In the nineteenth century canals were cut linking rivers to remote mining areas, thus making it possible for coal to be transported to the sea ports. Subsequently during the middle part of that century railways were built in every valley. This made transport so much easier. Industrial towns grew in the South Wales valleys as well as along the coast. In North Wales towns grew around the coal mining areas of the east and the slate quarry areas of the west.

Along the coast of Wales, especially in the west, a ship building industry developed which produced the vessels that carried Welsh slate and minerals to the far corners of the world.

recent history

Riots in Wales

The industrial areas attracted thousands of people from the impoverished countryside of Wales, but the problems arising from industrialisation were many. Poor housing conditions, poor working conditions and lack of understanding between workers and owners were common. Several riots occurred in Wales at the beginning of the nineteenth century both in the country and in the industrial towns. Many of these have been seen as uprisings of national and international significance.

The Merthyr Riots

The Merthyr Riots of 1831 were the most violent in the history of industry in Britain. Following the economic depression of 1829, workers complained about cuts in pay, and about lack of local government and parliamentary representation. At a time when workers' property was confiscated by courts, people were inspired by the new radical politics and workers formed their own union. The red flag was raised in a protest, possibly for the first time in Britain. A crowd of 10,000 iron workers faced 80 soldiers, resulting in 16 soldiers injured, and at least 24 of the crowd killed and 70 injured. The rebellion continued for a month. A force of Swansea Yeomanry was disarmed by the workers. Dic Penderyn, a 23 year old coal miner, was found guilty of wounding a Scottish soldier, and he was hanged in Cardiff prison. "O Arglwydd, dyma gamwedd" ("*O Lord, this is injustice*") were Dic's last words. Years later another man confessed to this act.

Port Talbot: The commemorative stone of Dic Penderyn, 1808-31, executed for his part to the Merthyr riots

The Chartist Insurrection

Between 1837 and 1844 many people were disillusioned by the lack of parliamentary reform and by the treatment of the poor. A Charter was drawn up calling for the vote for all men, constituencies equal in population size, an annual parliament, amongst other things. The movement was particularly strong in Wales, with the first revolt in Llanidloes, mid Wales, in April 1839. The Welsh Chartists marched on Newport in November 1839 hoping to take control of the town and start a nation-wide revolt. Around 20,000 men, most of them Welsh speakers from the surrounding valleys, took part, and fighting broke out at the Westgate Hotel, Newport. At least thirty were killed by English soldiers, with eight sentenced to be hanged and quartered. This was later commuted to imprisonment for five of them, a further three men, including the leader John Frost (1784-1877), being deported to Australia.

The Rebecca Riots

Toll gates had proliferated on roads owned by road trusts, particularly in west Wales, resulting in farmers having to pay for using vehicles and transporting

The Rebecca Riots

livestock and lime. The Rebecca Riots started on 13 May 1839 at Efail-wen on the border between Pembrokeshire and Carmarthenshire. The rioters dressed up in women's clothes, and took their name (Rebecca) from a verse in the Book of Genesis (ch.24, v.60). In these riots toll gates were demolished in an attempt to rid the roads of tolls. The riots, which were a remarkable example of a popular uprising and which eventually met with success, were a sign of wider discontent at the economic hardship and unfair government and administration. In 1843 the workhouse at Carmarthen was destroyed by rioters. The houses of unpopular justices of peace and those who raised unfair tithe payments were attacked. The keeper of a tollgate at Hendy was killed in 1843. The authorities sent 1,800 men to find the leaders. Five were deported to Australia in 1843. A Commission was set up to change the administration of roads in South Wales.

Welsh Banned in Schools

One result of the riots was that the English government thought the Welsh were prone to riot because of their lack of knowledge of English. Although Wales was largely nonconformist and Welsh speaking, three inspectors, all English Anglicans, were sent around Wales to report on the state of the teaching of English in schools in Wales. Their report of 1847 gave rise to what become known as the Treachery of the Blue Books. In the report they claimed that the Welsh language prevented the Welsh from taking a full part in the new industrial life, and stated that Welsh was only suitable for religion and poetry.

The report criticized school buildings, teaching resources and untrained teachers. Much of this was true, but they also attacked the Welsh for being lazy, superstitious, drunk and of loose morals.

The report became a crucial document in the anglicisation of Welsh education. In the Welsh press, the report was roundly condemned. However, with most industrial initiatives in the hands of English speaking owners and with English being seen as the language of the future, the Welsh in the last half of the nineteenth century strove to master English. Needless to say, this was at the expense of the Welsh language.

Most daily schools set up during this period were English schools. When primary education was made compulsory in Wales in 1870 Welsh was banned from the majority of schools. Pupils in all parts of Wales were punished for speaking Welsh in school. The anglicization of the education system, followed by massive immigration from England, changed the language patterns of Wales. Around 75% of the population spoke Welsh in 1851: 54% spoke Welsh in 1891.

Changing to English

English was the language of compulsory primary education in Wales in 1879 and it was also the language of the secondary schools. The Society for the Utilization of the Welsh Language was founded in 1885 with the aim of making Welsh an acceptable subject in schools, resulting in Welsh being made a secondary school subject in 1891.

At the same time, there was a strong movement to turn Welsh chapels into English ones, since it was thought that English was the language of the future. Members of Welsh chapels left their own chapels to start English ones.

More and more immigrants came to Wales to work in the coal industry, and most of these were English speaking. This, combined with English medium education, and the lack of confidence of the Welsh in their own language, caused English to become more and more influential.

The University of Wales

During the latter half of the nineteenth century, the Welsh successfully expanded the system of education available to Welsh people by setting up a college at Aberystwyth in 1872, at Bangor in 1883 and at Cardiff in 1884 and establishing the University of Wales in 1893. This was followed in the early years of the twentieth century by the establishment of the National Museum in Cardiff and the National Library at Aberystwyth in 1907. In keeping with the subservient attitude of the Welsh towards their own language, English was the only medium of education during the first quarter century of the University, at a time when national universities all over Europe were using their native languages. This did serious harm to the Welsh language as a language of education and as a national language.

Growth of Welsh Patriotism

At this time when Wales was becoming anglicized, many Welsh people tried to stem the tide. Some were inspired by the way many small nations in Europe were achieving self-government; others were inspired by the growth of Irish nationalism. Others were concerned to see a Welsh speaking country turning its back on the language. At the same time radical political ideas were becoming popular through the growth of the Liberal party, which advocated home rule for Wales. There was a growth of Welsh national feeling, and a desire to safeguard the language.

Michael D Jones (1822-1898), a firm supporter of self-government for Wales, who was born in the village of Llanuwchllyn near Bala, was responsible for establishing a Welsh colony in Patagonia, Argentina, so that the Welsh could have a country where the language of parliament, trade, science and education would be Welsh. At the time, thousands of Welsh people were emigrating to the United States of America. By the end of the nineteenth century there were 100,000 Welsh born people living there, and a total of around 400,000 of Welsh descent. Although many managed to live in Welsh societies, and set up Welsh chapels and other Welsh institutions (it is estimated that there were around 400 Welsh chapels in the states), it was fairly clear that it would be difficult for Welsh to survive there. The colony in Patagonia was started in 1865 and, although the aim was never really achieved, there is still a society of Welsh speakers in Patagonia.

Dan Issac Davies (1839-1887) from Llanymddyfri

Michael D. Jones

(Llandovery) was one of the founders of the first Welsh Language Society which succeeded in ensuring that the secondary education act of 1891 allowed Welsh to be taught as a school subject.

Owen M Edwards (1858-1920), also of Llanuwchllyn, was punished for speaking Welsh at school when he was a child. He became a Fellow of Lincoln College, Oxford, but devoted his life to writing Welsh history, publishing Welsh literature and producing Welsh magazines. He published the latter with the purpose of giving Welsh people a knowledge of their own history and literature which they were prevented from gaining at school. His magazine for children sold 12,000 copies a month at the beginning of the 20th century. He also aimed at setting up a Welsh medium youth organisation, an aim that was achieved by his son, Ifan ab Owen Edwards. Owen M Edwards, who had been a Liberal member of parliament for a short while, became chief inspector of schools in Wales and ensured that Welsh could be used as a medium of education.

Emrys ap Iwan (1851-1906) believed in self-government for Wales and advocated using Welsh in courts and in trading. He was a literary critic and political writer. He fiercely attacked the movement that aimed at anglicizing Welsh chapels, but his main influence was on the early nationalists of the twentieth century.

The main movement that advocated self government for Wales was the Young Wales Movement, formed in 1886 as part of the Liberal party. Its leaders included T E Ellis of Bala, who was a member of parliament and Liberal Whip, and David Lloyd George, who became Prime Minister in 1916. A split in the Liberal Party in Wales caused this movement to come to a close in 1896. Its secretary had been Beriah Gwynfe Evans (1848-1927) who was also the first secretary of the Welsh Language Society. He was a journalist, novelist, playwright and producer of a popular literary magazine.

David Lloyd George

The Eisteddfod

Welsh culture in the second half of the nineteenth century was being promoted by several eisteddfodau, the main one being the National Eisteddfod, which was first held in 1858. It developed to be Wales' foremost cultural institution. In 1819 the druidic order, inspired by Iolo Morganwg, was linked to the eisteddfod.

Hundreds of small eisteddfodau (which include singing, reciting, bardic, cultural and competitions) are still held throughout Wales. The Urdd (National Youth Movement of Wales) holds an annual eisteddfod for young people which lasts a week. This is held alternately in north and south Wales and is claimed to be the largest youth festival in Europe. The National Eisteddfod of Wales also lasts a week and follows a similar pattern.

At the National Eisteddfod, the main prize for poetry written in the traditional strict pattern is a chair (symbolic of the poet's importance in the courts of the kings) and the main prize for poetry not written in this

Later Industrialisation

As coal, iron and copper deposits were mined, parts of Wales became highly industrialised in the nineteenth century. The iron works of Dowlais and Merthyr Tudful and the copper works at Swansea contributed to the general wealth of Britain. By 1913, South Wales was responsible for a third of the world's coal exports. The development of coal mines employed 270,000 men and women in 1919. But at the end of the era of heavy industry, Wales was left with large derelict areas, high unemployment levels, and little wealth to show for the exploitation of its minerals. Wales had been treated by England as a colony, its cheap labour supply and its abundance of minerals having fuelled the British Empire.

Rhondda, the valley known all over the world for its coal, had a population of 951 in 1851. By 1881 it had grown to 55,000. Most of these people were Welsh country people, who had come from the poverty of west and north Wales to seek work. It has been argued that the development of iron works and coal mines in South Wales saved the Welsh language: the Welsh did not have to emigrate to America in huge numbers as the Irish did. Welsh was the main language of most of

Children taking part in the Urdd (Welsh League of Youth) Eisteddfod

strict pattern is a crown. There are main prizes for prose writers, singers, choirs, visual artists and others. The decision that Welsh would be the only language used in the national eisteddfod was taken in 1937 to safeguard the eisteddfod as a Welsh cultural institution.

A former mining village in the Afan valley, where trees once again beautify the landscape

the iron, coal and copper workers in Wales at this time. Between 1900 and 1910 130,000 people immigrated to Wales, but even in 1921, 45% of the population of Glamorgan could still speak Welsh.

The industrial expansion continued. Merthyr, Swansea, Newport and Cardiff became large industrial towns. By 1924 Rhondda had a population of 167,000. At the end of the nineteenth century and the beginning of the twentieth century, more and more people came into South Wales from England and other countries. This contributed greatly to the anglicisation of South Wales.

The development of industry in North and South Wales led to the development of trade unions which later became an important part of Welsh political life.

There are today only one or two thousand coal miners in Wales, working mainly in small private mines. Coal is today mainly extracted from large open cast sites. A notable exception is the Tower Colliery near Hirwaun, South Wales, where workers have successfully taken over the running of the pit.

In the second half of the twentieth century, the industrial face of Wales was transformed. The coal mining era came to an end, and the steel works at Port Talbot, Trostre and Newport were slimmed down.

Unemployment as a result of these changes has remained constantly high. Between 1979 and 1997 the Government in London changed the ways of counting the number of unemployed more than twenty times, but even so, some 10% of the Welsh workforce is usually unemployed. Cardiff has developed as a financial and professional centre. Heavy industry has given way in the valleys to factories producing parts for cars and television sets. Most of these factories are owned by corporations in America, Germany and the Far East.

The Welsh Development Agency, set up in 1976, has helped clear the landscape of tips, provided accommodation for factories and attracted many foreign companies. They have succeeded partly because of the low wage structure in Wales and the high unemployment levels following the collapse of the heavy industries.

Agriculture still thrives but with a diminishing labour force. The emphasis in many places is on the service industries and many jobs today are part time or short term, especially in areas depending on tourism.

Growth of Socialism

Keir Hardie (1856-1915), the Scotsman who was elected MP for Merthyr Tudful, was the first Labour Member of Parliament in Britain. He was in favour of Welsh home rule and was also a lay preacher but apart from preacher-poet-communist T E Nicholas (1878-1971) the main promotors of the new socialism in Wales were English speaking,

The Labour Party took the place of the Welsh Liberal Party as Wales' main political party and was aided by the strength of trade unions in Wales. Some of the most influential of these, such as the Union of Quarrymen in North Wales and the Union of Coal Miners in the south, were Welsh institutions. The South Wales Miners' Federation had been founded in 1889. Although many chapels preached a social religion, the new socialism developed separately. Instead of following its early ideals it quickly became a British imperialist party, so that when it came to power after the First World War, little mention was made of home rule for Wales and the Welsh language was given scant attention. The Labour Party has been accused of turning its back on the Welsh language at a time when it could have contributed positively to its survival.

During the socialist awakening, Miners' Institutes were set up throughout the South Wales valleys. These housed libraries and gave workers an opportunity to extend their knowledge and education as well as providing leisure activities.

Strikes and Riots

There were many strikes in the quarrying industry in North Wales and in the mining industry in South Wales, most of which concerned pay and working conditions; others concerned the recognition of trade unions. There had been several strikes and lock-outs at the turn of the century in the quarries of Caernarfonshire where the longest dispute, at Penrhyn quarry, lasted from 1900 to 1903. In the south, 100,000 miners were locked out for six months in 1898, and this led to the foundation of the South Wales Miners' Federation, with Mabon (William Abraham, 1842-1922) as president. Several strikes took place in the Rhondda, and in 1910 there was rioting at Tonypandy where one man was killed in fighting between police and workers after Winston Churchill sent in soldiers to patrol the area. At a railwaymen's strike at Llanelli in 1911, troops killed two workers; in 1912 there was a national strike.

Working class solidarity in a miners' strike of the 1980s

The national miners' strike of 1926 led to the General Strike, when the Welsh miners refused to work for months, until their poverty and starvation forced them to return. The Welsh miners had nevertheless been let down by the TUC which called off the General Strike after a week. Having committed themselves to a British socialism, Welsh workers found that they could not depend on support from England.

The number of coal mines diminished gradually from this time onwards, and scores of pits were closed during the 1960s and 1970s by both Conservative and Labour governments. The coal miners' strike of the 1980s followed the heroic attempts of coal miners and their families to keep their communities alive but the end of this strike signalled the end of the coal mining era in Wales.

Coal Mining Disasters

The lack of concern for workers' safety as well as difficult geological conditions caused frequent underground disasters. 268 miners were killed at Abercarn, south-east Wales, in 1878, 290 miners were killed at Albion Colliery, Cilfynydd in 1894. In 1913, 439 men were killed in a disaster at Senghennydd and in 1934, 265 miners were killed at Gresford colliery, north-east Wales. Smaller disasters occurred at regular intervals, not to mention the regular fatal accidents. A tragic legacy of the coal mining era was the collapse of the tip at Aberfan, which engulfed the village school in 1966, killing 144 people, including 116 children. This was cruel confirmation of the way in which South Wales people had been exploited by the coal industry.

First World War

The first World War, 1914-1918, had a devastating effect on the Welsh language. The Welsh had been slow to enlist at the outset, but Lloyd George whipped up support, using chapel ministers who preached dressed up in army uniform. 280,000 Welshmen fought in the war, 40,000 of whom died. Wales had thus lost almost 10% of its Welsh-speaking men. The horror of the war came to a climax in the Battle of the Somme, when 420,000 British soldiers died, 19,000 of them on the first day. The Welsh Division played a prominent part in this campaign. One poet, Hedd Wyn (Ellis Humphrey Evans), who won the chair – the main prize for poetry – at the National Eisteddfod at Birkenhead in 1917, died in battle before knowing of his success. The chair which should have been his was draped in a black mantle, and this particular eisteddfod has been known since as 'Eisteddfod y Gadair Ddu' (*The Eisteddfod of the Black Chair*).

Many Welshmen who took part in this war, supposedly to defend the small countries of Europe, felt that Wales had lost out as a result of it. Many became ardent pacifists and others committed themselves to the defence of Wales. Among them were Saunders Lewis and Lewis Valentine who were among the founders of Plaid Cymru, the Welsh National Party.

The Labour Party in Wales

In the 1918 elections, ten Labour MPs were elected from Wales, all of whom had been in favour of the imperialist world war which had just been fought. When the Labour Party shortly afterwards formed the government, it failed to support home rule for Wales. The efforts of the last forty years to give Wales home rule had come to nothing.

Aneurin Bevan

The one great figure to emerge from the Labour Party in Wales was Aneurin Bevan (1897-1960), born at Tredegar, Gwent, the son of a Welsh speaking Baptist father. Typical of the supposedly international Marxist stance of the day (which really meant embracing England) he refused to act to protect Welsh identity, but will be remembered for his contribution to the welfare state. It is no coincidence that it was another Welshman, Lloyd George, who introduced old age pensions and national insurance.

The Labour Party has remained the main political party in Wales throughout the century. In 1964 it began to devolve power to Wales from London by setting up the Welsh Office with a Secretary of State for Wales. Although it formally supported the formation of a Welsh Assembly in 1979, most of its members campaigned against it, led by such English orientated MPs as Neil Kinnock, Leo Abse and George Thomas. Wales became one of the very few European nations to refuse a measure of home rule. By the end of the 1990s however, after more than fifteen years of damaging Conservative rule in Wales, the Labour Party supported the setting up of a Welsh Assembly which would take over the responsibilities of the Welsh Office. These responsibilities include housing, roads, industrial development, education and many other fields which

A statue of Aneurin Bevan at the top of Queen Street, Cardiff

are currently under the administration of unelected committees.

In the General Election of 1997, no Conservative MPs were returned from Wales. Plaid Cymru had 4 MPs and Liberal Democrats 2. One of the first acts of the new Labour Government was to arrange another referendum on the issue of setting up a Welsh Assembly.

Economic Depression

The economic depression, which began in 1925, had a devastating effect on Wales. Because of unemployment and poverty, 500,000 people emigrated from Wales between 1921 and 1939. 259,000 people left the South Wales valleys. In August 1932, 42.8% of insured men in Wales were unemployed, while in some areas, such as Merthyr Tudful, the percentage was much higher. The economic depression affected all western countries, but its effect in Wales was particularly severe and more long lasting, as the foreign markets for coal, on which Wales depended, collapsed. This has had a huge effect on Welsh society and the Welsh language. The coal mining valleys of South Wales have not really recovered, and unemployment levels are still grotesquely high in many parts.

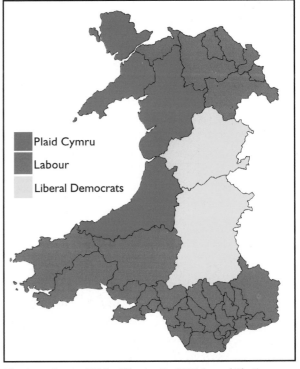

Plaid Cymru

Labour

Liberal Democrats

The electoral map of Wales following the 1997 General Election

The Second World War

The disruption of Welsh society continued immediately after the depression, with the start of the Second World War. Around 15,000 Welsh soldiers were killed in this war, which killed 30 million globally. The centre of Swansea was demolished in 1941 by fire-bombs and more than 11,000 houses were damaged; 369 people died in 44 air raids on the town. In Cardiff, 30,000 houses were damaged. The cultural life of Wales suffered immensely because of the war, and this caused yet more harm to the already precarious state of the Welsh language.

200,000 people moved into Wales from England during the first two years of the war, and Wales was used as a centre for evacuees, mainly children from English cities. Some nationalists had argued that Wales should have been neutral during this war, and there was a greater proportion of conscientious objectors in Wales than in England.

The devastation of the bombing on Swansea

Plaid Cymru – The National Party of Wales

Plaid Cymru was established in 1925 because the founders realised that the English parties would not give Wales home rule nor act positively to safeguard the Welsh language. Although Plaid Cymru has only succeeded in having four members of parliament at any one time during the 1990s, it has nevertheless influenced the politics of Wales throughout the century, not least by causing all the English political parties to establish Welsh sections.

All political parties have given support for the Welsh language during the last 25 years of the 20th century and all except the Conservatives have advocated a measure of home rule for Wales. Plaid Cymru can claim that many of Wales' political and administrative institutions and establishments have come about through its pressure.

The 1979 referendum result on Welsh home rule, which would have given Wales a Welsh Assembly to decide on internal affairs, was a great disappointment to Plaid Cymru. A majority of around 4-1 voted against the proposal. This was followed by 18 years of centralist Conservative government, so when the

Cardiff Bay, the location of the new National Assembly for Wales building – the first Welsh government in over 500 years

Labour Party returned to power in London in 1997, it supported a Welsh Assembly to a greater degree than it did in 1979. The 1997 referendum on Welsh Home

rule resulted in a 51%-49% vote in favour, and the National Assembly for Wales, the first all Wales political establishment since the early 1400s, was given the go-ahead, with a starting date of 1999.

During its early years, Plaid Cymru was influential in securing a radio service for Wales, and through the symbolic bombing of a school for training bomber pilots in Llŷn, North Wales, in 1936, it won mass support for the first time. Its campaign for full status for Welsh, however, led only to the Welsh Courts Act of 1942, which gave limited powers to use Welsh in court. Other campaigns by Plaid Cymru involved opposition to the use of land in Wales by the War Ministry.

One of the main campaigns after the war was the struggle against the drowning of Capel Celyn, a Welsh speaking village near Bala, North Wales. The campaign was in vain: the valley was drowned in 1965 to give water to Liverpool. The drowning of this small Welsh speaking community, which had almost unanimous political support from all in Wales, came to symbolise how defenceless Wales was in the face of continuing English oppression.

It was no coincidence that Plaid Cymru won its first parliamentary seat, in Carmarthen, in 1966 and came close to winning several seats in industrial South Wales. Concessions made to Wales following this show of support for Plaid Cymru included the building of motorways in Wales, establishing a motor vehicle tax centre in Swansea, and growing support for the Welsh language.

Saunders Lewis

Saunders Lewis(1893-1985) was one of the most influential figures of the early Plaid Cymru. A founder and president of the party, he was also the century's main Welsh dramatist, as well as being a renowned poet and literary critic. His policies included opposing international capitalism and state control, and he argued in favour of a co-operative economic system. He had high hopes that Plaid Cymru would sweep the country, but his economic policy of deindustrialising South Wales was unrealistic. He came nearest to gaining mass support after he was imprisoned for burning the bomber pilot training school with D J Williams, a teacher and short story writer, and Lewis Valentine, a Baptist minister, in Llŷn in 1936. Saunders Lewis lost his lecturing post at Swansea, and the banning of Welsh in the court case earned him and his cause much sympathy. But the advent of the second world war cut short any hopes that Plaid Cymru had of achieving quick success for Welsh nationalism.

Gwynfor Evans

Gwynfor Evans (1912-), a native of Barry, became Plaid Cymru's president in 1945 and he led the party until 1981. He became the party's first member of parliament in 1966, when he won a by-election in Carmarthen. He has written prolifically, including many books on Welsh history, believing that Wales cannot be a nation without knowing its history.

He will also be remembered for his part in securing a Welsh language television channel. When, in 1979, the Conservative government withdrew its promise to set up a channel that would broadcast Welsh programmes during peak hours, he threatened to fast to death. The fear of a subsequent national revolution caused the government to set up the channel S4C.

Dafydd Wigley

During the 1990s, Dafydd Wigley (1943-), a member of parliament for Caernarfon since the 70s, was Plaid Cymru's president. He has campaigned strenuously for home rule, as well as for other Welsh issues, including equality of status for Welsh and the right for Welsh education, the expansion of the Welsh economy, and for social issues such as compensation for quarrymen and provision for the disabled.

Urdd Gobaith Cymru
(*The Welsh League of Youth*)

This movement, which claims more than 50,000 members, was founded by Ifan ab Owen Edwards (1895-1970), the son of Owen Edwards, in 1922. It has two large youth camps, at Llangrannog in Ceredigion and at Glanllyn near Bala, where young people can enjoy themselves using Welsh. It also organises an annual national eisteddfod for young people which is the climax of competitions in hundreds of smaller eisteddfodau. Its main aim is to promote the Welsh language among children and young people, and a lot of its work is concentrated on schools. It produces magazines for Welsh speakers and learners and organises various events and youth clubs in many parts of Wales.

The Urdd magazine stand at the annual eisteddfod

Cymdeithas yr Iaith Gymraeg (The Welsh Language Society)

In 1962 Saunders Lewis felt that Plaid Cymru had failed to achieve its objective of saving the Welsh language. At that time it had not won a single parliamentary seat. In a BBC lecture he called on Plaid Cymru members to use unconstitutional methods so that it would be impossible to carry out the administration of government in the Welsh speaking areas of Wales without using Welsh. It was Cymdeithas yr Iaith Gymraeg, which was established in that year, rather than Plaid Cymru, which started this campaign. It operates all over Wales, not only in areas with a majority of Welsh speakers.

It has successfully fought many campaigns which included painting roadsigns, taking English only leaflets from public offices and holding sit-ins in television studios. Hundreds of its members have been fined and imprisoned as a result of their actions. Bilingual road signs became compulsory in 1971 after the society had painted and removed English only signs. In 1967 a Welsh Language Act was passed with the aim of promoting the official use of the language. Many public bodies, including the Post Office, started using Welsh. In 1982 S4C, the partly Welsh television channel, was set up after many members had been imprisoned for disrupting broadcasting. In 1993 another Welsh Language Act was passed with the aim of giving Welsh equality with English and ensuring that all public bodies have a bilingual policy. This is remarkable progress. It is now difficult to imagine the Wales of the 1960s where Welsh was to all intents and purposes banned as an official language.

Welsh and the Law

The Act of Annexation of 1536 had banned the official use of Welsh in courts. This was the position until 1942. As a result of a petition of 500,000 calling for equal status for Welsh, the Welsh Courts Act was passed in 1942, but this only gave a Welsh speaker the right to use Welsh if he would be under a disadvantage if he used English. As recently as 1967, Judge Widgery said that Welsh should not be given greater status in Wales than Polish. Nevertheless, the 1967 Welsh Language Act gave Welsh speakers the right to use Welsh in courts. The 1993 Welsh Language Act has ordered courts to operate a bilingual policy that will give Welsh speakers equal rights, but there is still no right to have a Welsh speaking jury.

A Cymdeithas yr Iaith demonstration for a Welsh Language Act in central L[...]

Welsh Education

Although the Welsh Department of the Education Board had encouraged the use of Welsh in primary schools in Welsh speaking areas as early as 1907, many parts of the country were slow to respond, and there were no Welsh schools in English speaking parts of Wales.

In 1939 Ifan ab Owen Edwards started a private Welsh school in Aberystwyth and, in 1947, the first Welsh school under a local authority was set up in Llanelli. The first secondary school to use Welsh as a medium of education was set up in Rhyl in 1956. The Welsh Joint Education Committee was established in 1949.

Today there are almost 500 primary schools which teach through the medium of Welsh, and more than 50 secondary schools. More than 25% of Welsh primary schools now teach mainly through the medium of Welsh. More than 30,000 pupils are considered fluent in Welsh, and more than half of these come from English speaking homes. Counties in north and west Wales ensure that most of their schools teach mainly through the medium of Welsh, and there are Welsh medium schools in all parts south and east Wales as well. Welsh education is available to children from all homes, both Welsh and English speaking. All children, of course, are taught English to a high standard, and the Welsh schools have earned a reputation for providing higher than average standards of education.

Most secondary schools in Wales are comprehensive, and there are in Wales comparatively few private (wrongly called 'public') schools. Most of these secondary schools, which do not teach through the medium of Welsh, now teach Welsh as a second language.

Mudiad Ysgolion Meithrin
(Welsh Nursery Schools Movement)

The Welsh nursery schools movement was established in 1971 to organise the work already done in many Welsh nursery groups throughout the country. It receives funding from the government, and it organises nursery groups for children under school age from Welsh and English speaking homes. This gives young children an advantage when they start school, and it is the perfect age to learn a language. In 1995 the movement had 624 nursery groups which attracted 15,097 children of whom more than half came from English speaking homes.

Children at Ysgol Gymraeg Lôn-las – Swansea's first Welsh medium primary school, established in 1949

Civic Buildings, Cardiff

1893	University of Wales
1907	Charter for National Museum, Cardiff (opened 1922)
1907	Charter for National Library, Aberystwyth (opened 1916)
1919	Welsh Health Board
1920	Board of Celtic Studies
1922	Welsh University Press
1928	Welsh National Symphony Orchestra
1945	Welsh National Opera Company
1947	Welsh Folk Museum, St. Fagans
1948	Welsh Gas Board
1951	Minister for Welsh Affairs
1952	BBC Council for Wales
1960	Welsh 'Grand' Committee
1961	Welsh Books Council
1964	Welsh Office
1972	Welsh Sports Council
1973	Wales TUC
1975	Welsh Labour Party
1975	Welsh Consumer Council
1976	Welsh Development Agency
1977	Development Board for Rural Wales
1978	Welsh CBI
1982	S4C – partly Welsh television channel
1984	Cadw (Heritage in Wales)
1988	Welsh Language Board
1991	Countryside Council for Wales
1999	National Assembly for Wales

Welsh Institutions

The growth of Welsh institutions during the twentieth century has been remarkable. By today a vast amount of the political, economic, cultural and sporting life of Wales is organised on Welsh national lines. On the left is a table showing some of the main institutions created over the last century.

Welsh Publishing

Although Welsh publishing had its golden age in the nineteenth century, Welsh literature, Welsh books and magazines have thrived throughout most of the twentieth century. Although only 50 books a year were published around 1950, today between 400 and 500 titles are published in Welsh every year. The government started giving grants to Welsh books in 1956. The growth is due in part to the subsidy received by publishers through the Welsh Books Council established in 1961, which is supported by the government and local authorities. The Council is also responsible for commissioning books and for help with editing and marketing. The books produced include school text books, many children's books, novels, poetry, and general titles. Around 50 publishers are in business, and the biggest printer-publishers are Gwasg Gomer (based in Llandysul, Ceredigion), Y Lolfa (Talybont, Ceredigion) and Carreg Gwalch (Llanrwst). Magazines published in Welsh include the weekly news magazine, *Golwg*, and the weekly paper *Y Cymro*. Monthlies include around 50 regional newspapers (*papurau bro*), produced voluntarily in all parts of Wales. Between them they are read by 250,000 people.

There are also, of course, many publishers who publish English-language books in Wales.

Poets and Authors

Scores of authors write in Welsh today and they are contributing to one of the richest centuries for Welsh writing. They include many women such as novelists Angharad Tomos, Meg Ellis, Eigra Lewis Roberts and Jane Edwards, poets Menna Elfyn and Einir Jones. Other recent writers include the manager of Portmeirion village in North Wales, Robin Llywelyn, who has won the prose medal at the National Eisteddfod. Mihangel Morgan writes witty, surrealist short stories; Twm Morys is a popular singer and an itinerant poet; Myrddin ap Dafydd, Iwan Llwyd, Emyr

Lewis and Meirion McIntyre Huws are young poets expert in the traditional cynghanedd. Poetry has always been the main literary form in Wales, but the short story and the novel have been prominent in the twentieth century. Well known twentieth century Welsh language authors include the following:

T Gwynn Jones (1871-1949) prolific poet, using themes from Celtic mythology, and concern for civilisation

Kate Roberts (1891-1985) short stories and novels depicting hardship of quarrymen and women of North Wales

T E Nicholas (1878-1971) socialist poet

Gwenallt (David James Jones, 1899-1968) from Swansea valley; imprisoned as a pacifist; nationalist, socialist and Christian poet

T H Parry-Williams (1887-1975) poet, on Snowdonia and life

T Rowland Hughes (1903-1949) poet and novelist; wrote five novels during his long last illness, mainly on the deterioration of the slate industry

Waldo Williams (1904-1971) from Pembrokeshire; imprisoned as a pacifist; a visionary poet

Saunders Lewis (1893-1985) brought up in Liverpool's Welsh society; novelist and poet, but mainly known as a dramatist, using many themes, especially from Welsh history and mythology.

Rhydwen Williams (1916-1997) poet and novelist, whose main works depict life in the Rhondda and other mining valleys

Marian Eames (1921-) novelist on historic themes

Islwyn Ffowc Elis (1924-) popular novels on many aspects of Welsh life

R Williams Parry (1884-1956) poet, on nature, people and life

Dic Jones (1934-) farmer-poet from Ceredigion

Gwyn Thomas (1936-) poet, on modern civilisation and life

Gerallt Lloyd Owen (1944-) poet, nationalist and historic themes

English-Language Literature

Because of the wealth of the Welsh literary tradition, many were unwilling to recognise English-language writers in Wales, especially as many of the early prominent ones, such as Caradoc Evans (1878-1945) and Gwyn Thomas (1913-1981) were antagonistic to Welsh society or the Welsh language. However, many works depicting the industrial life of South Wales were written by Jack Jones (1884-1970), Lewis Jones (1897-1939), Rhys Davies (1903-1978), Idris Davies (1905-1953) and others. The most widely read modern author is Iris Gower, from Swansea, whose books concentrate on the industrial life of Swansea in the last century. Other authors include the poets Dylan Thomas (1914-1953) and Vernon Watkins (1906-1967), both of Swansea. Harri Webb (1920-1995), also from Swansea, was a very popular Welsh nationalist poet writing mainly in English. Younger prolific writers include Nigel Jenkins, again from the Swansea area. R S Thomas (1913-) is now considered to be the greatest poet writing in English. Many of his poems are religious and others depict the crises facing Wales. His work has ensured that English-language writing is now accepted as another facet of Welsh culture.

Nigel Jenkins

Broadcasting In Wales

A protest in the early 80's campaigning for a Welsh-language channel

Saunders Lewis called for a radio service for Wales in 1931. Eventually, a Welsh region of the BBC was established in 1937. Some Welsh television broadcasts started in 1952, but most Welsh programmes were late at night. By 1962, the BBC provided 6 hours of Welsh TV a week and a similar number of hours was provided by independent companies. Following years of campaigning, S4C was established in 1982, and it provides around 30 hours of Welsh a week, mostly during peak viewing hours. With the advent of digital television, this will expand to an all day Welsh service. The government grants a £50 million subsidy to this channel. S4C's programmes are supplied by the BBC, HTV (the independent service in Wales) and around 50 small independent companies provide the rest of the Welsh output. One of S4C's most popular programmes is Pobol y Cwm (*People of the Valley*), a nightly soap opera.

The BBC provides an almost all day Welsh radio service, and other smaller companies, such as Radio Ceredigion and Swansea Sound, provide some Welsh service.

'Derek' and 'Karen' who run the garage in Pobol y Cwm (photograph courtesy of S4C)

Ieuan Evans, former captain of the Welsh rugby team

Sport

Wales has also achieved a separate identity in the world of sport. The Football Association of Wales was formed in 1876, and the Welsh Rugby Union in 1881. This was followed by the formation of Welsh national associations for other sports, including hockey (1890), golf (1895),

swimming (1897), gymnastics (1902), bowling (1904), boxing (1910) and athletics (1948). Wales has a national athletics team in the Commonwealth games. Wales has national teams in all these sports, and is recognized worldwide as a separate country in sport. Much of Wales' feeling of national identity is today expressed through its national sporting teams, some of whose members become national heroes, such as Colin Jackson, the record breaking hurdler.

Recent famous names include Ian Woosnam (golf), Ian Rush and Ryan Giggs (football), Terry Griffiths (snooker), Johnny Owen (boxing), Gareth Edwards and Ieuan Evans (rugby), Tony Lewis and Robert Croft (cricket), Lynn Davies (athletics).

Welsh Choirs, Clubs and Movements

Wales has a wealth of choirs which include male voice and mixed choirs, women's choirs and youth choirs. Many of the choirs are associated with chapels, while others are linked to rugby clubs or villages and towns. Famous choirs include Llanelli male voice, Treorci male voice, and Morriston Orpheus choirs in South Wales, and Rhos and Godre'r Aran in North Wales. Some Welsh choirs specialise in *penillion* singing, where the accompanying melody, often on the harp, is harmonised by the singers.

Wales also has an enormous number of rugby and football clubs. These proliferate in all parts of Wales, with rugby clubs more popular in the south and football in the north. Cardiff, Swansea, Llanelli, Neath and Pontypridd are regarded as the main rugby clubs, but others can compete well with them. Swansea, Cardiff and Wrexham play football in the main English leagues, but Wales has its own national league which has gained in influence in recent years. Barry, Caernarfon and Bangor are among the strongest teams in this league.

Several cricket clubs are also popular. Glamorgan County, which plays against the English counties, has its centre at Cardiff but it also plays at Swansea and elsewhere.

Many of these clubs are not only sporting clubs but also social clubs and, as such, are social centres for the various towns and villages which they serve. Recently Welsh language clubs have been established. Clwb Ifor Bach in Cardiff, Clwb y Bont in Pontypridd and Tŷ Tawe in Swansea are examples. These arrange evenings for learners as well as other social events.

Tŷ Tawe youth choir, Swansea

Although the chapel population is diminishing, the chapels retain their influence and are to be found in all towns and many smaller communities.

There are more Welsh language courses held for learners of Welsh than ever before. The Wlpan courses, varying in length and intensity, are organised mainly by the University of Wales, while other courses are organised by centres of adult education (usually in schools or colleges) throughout Wales. Some 15,000 people attend these courses every year.

Every town and village has a branch of Merched y Wawr (*Women of the Dawn*), a movement for Welsh speaking women, while many towns have a Clwb Cinio (*Dining Club*) for Welsh speaking men.

Other organisations which further Welsh culture include folk dancing clubs, dramatic societies, bardic teams for which competitions are regularly organised, as well as brass bands and other musical institutions.

Evenings of Welsh entertainment, Noson Lawen, which include *penillion* singing, folk singing and folk dancing, are held in many towns throughout the year, often for the sake of visitors. Hymn singing festivals, *Gymanfa Ganu*, are held at various times of the year but especially around Easter.

Unrest

Wales has never followed the military option seen in Ireland and in many countries world wide. The nationalist movement has generally been a pacifist one.

Even the activist Cymdeithas yr Iaith Gymraeg (*The Welsh Language Society*) has always adhered to a commitment to non-violence.

Violence to property, however, has been resorted to, at times. When the dam at Capel Celyn was being built to provide water for Liverpool, several explosions occurred. This was the time that the Free Wales Army,

Caernarfon – the location of great nationalist unrest during the 1969 investiture of Prince Charles in the castle

largely a publicity group, was formed. More serious were the activities of MAC (Meibion Amddiffyn Cymru – *Sons in Defence of Wales*). Pipelines, tax offices and other material targets were struck. Two died at Abergele in an attempt to destroy a railway line that would take the royal family to the investiture at Caernarfon in 1969. John Jenkins, who was responsible for many explosions, was jailed for 10 years.

More recently, in view of the Government's inability to curb the growth of holiday homes in north and west Wales, homes which were bought by outsiders thus excluding local people, the movement called Meibion Glyndŵr (*Sons of Glyndŵr*) burnt scores of cottages. Only one has been caught, suggesting a high degree of local support for this kind of action.

Angler's Retreat, a holiday home in mid-Wales, burnt to the ground

customs

Many of the folk customs associated with various parts of Wales are similar to customs in other parts of Europe. Some old Welsh customs were eradicated by the religious revivals that Wales has experienced but attempts have been made to revive them.

Y Fari Lwyd (*The Grey Mary or Mare*)

One custom involves parading the head of a horse around the houses of a village or town as part of the new year's ceremonies. The head of the horse will already have been dug up after being buried in lime. With a cloak attached to it, it is worn by the leader of a group of people who take part in a verse recitation competition with the home dwellers. The aim of the revellers is to gain entry into the house to share drink and food.

Plygain (*Dawn carol service*)

The singing of carols at a dawn service ('plygain') was popular in many parts of Wales, and has been revived. It involved staying up all night at Christmas, or getting up very early, as the service could start at 3 a.m. Before the service young people would make 'cyflaith' (*treacle toffee*) and would be generally very merry by the start of the service. The carols sung at *plygain* are still popular.

Y Fari Lwyd – a custom which is still very much alive in Cowbridge, Vale of Glamorgan Photograph: Emlyn Phillips

Dydd Calan (*New Year's Day*)

The first day of the year ('dydd Calan') was more important than Christmas. Children would go from house to house wishing health and prosperity to the inhabitants. They carried a decorated apple or orange to symbolize their wish. Verses were sung and the children received gifts, called 'calennig', usually in the form of money, fruit or sweets.

Dydd Calan Hen (*Old New Year's Day*)

Parts of Pembrokeshire still celebrate the 'old' new year in the middle of January, with feasting and general merriment among adults and children, who are given a day off school. The celebration of the Old New Year's Day started in 1752 when the calendar was changed, with farmers keeping to this date to give those who helped them with the harvest a feast on the Old New Year's Day.

Llwyau Caru (*Love spoons*)

It was men, rather than women, who gave tokens of their feelings. These included giving love spoons, which were carved of wood. They included many symbols such as keys, hearts, anchors, houses as well as the initials of the lovers. The stems were sometimes hollowed, allowing small wooden balls (from the same piece of wood) to run in the cavity. These could symbolize the number of children wished for. Carving love spoons today has become a commercial business.

Calan Mai (*1st of May*)

May Day was celebrated by singing May carols around the houses. This then led to feasting. Dancing around the maypole was popular in some areas, although in some parts of the country a pole of birch ('y fedwen haf') would be raised at midsummer. Both celebrations involved dancing around the pole, sometimes in various states of undress.

Harvesting

The help given by neighbouring farmers and servants to each other at harvest time led to many customs. A day of harvesting would end in a special supper, followed by dancing and games. One custom involved preparing a 'caseg fedi' (*harvest mare*) which consisted of the last tufts of corn. This would be left standing, and the reapers, at a distance of between twenty and forty yards, would throw their reaping hooks at it. The 'mare' would be carried into the house, but women preparing the feast would hinder entry. This led to much horse-play.

Dydd Gŵyl Ddewi
(*St David's Day, March 1st*)

St David (Dewi) is the patron saint of Wales. He died in the year 589, and March 1st was either the date of his birth or death. The day is celebrated throughout Wales by wearing daffodils or leeks. Schools throughout the country organise concerts and eisteddfodau and girls wear the national costume. Attempts are being made to revive the custom of giving schools and other institutions a day or a half day holiday on the saint's day.

St David's Cathedral

Y Ddraig Goch (*The Red Dragon*)

It is probable that the Roman soldiers introduced the dragon to Britain and in time the Red Dragon became the heraldic symbol of Wales, as seen on the national flag. It is first mentioned in *Historia Brittonum*, attributed to Nennius around 800 AD. In it a tale is related concerning the battle between a red dragon and a white dragon which fought underground. According to tradition Arthur carried the Red Dragon after his father Uthr Bendragon had seen a dragon in the sky as a sign that he would be king. Poets often compared the Welsh princes to dragons and Owain Glyndŵr carried a yellow dragon on a white background when he attacked Caernarfon castle in 1401. The dragon became a popular symbol when it was used on the coat of arms of Henry VII when he won the battle of Bosworth, 1485. In 1807 it became the royal symbol for Wales, and it has since been used as a national symbol.

Museum of Welsh Life

The Museum of Welsh Life at St Fagans near Cardiff was opened in 1948. It includes a large collection of old buildings from all parts of Wales as well as a large number of artefacts connected with Welsh rural and urban life. Its activities also include collecting information on Welsh life, customs and language and it organises special events to celebrate some of the old festival days.

tales

Wales abounds in tales of many kinds. Some are tales of magic, where wishes come true and where the impossible can be accomplished. Fairies and even ants come to the help of men. Other tales are connected with the supernatural, and in these magicians, witches and mythological animals cast spells. A large number of tales are associated with historic figures, such as Arthur, Owain Glyndŵr, and Twm Siôn Cati, the 16th century highwayman. Other tales aim at provoking humour. Many tales are associated with lakes or hills, and many survive from prehistoric times. Some tales involve giants while others concern saints and religion. Here is a very brief selection.

Dwynwen

Saint Dwynwen, whose day is celebrated on January 25th as the festival day for Welsh lovers, was in love with Maelon, but her father had arranged her marriage to another prince. Maelon in anger raped Dwynwen who in grief prayed to God to relieve her of her love for Maelon. She was granted three wishes by God. Her first wish was for Maelon, who had been turned into ice by an angel, to be unfrozen. Her second wish was for God to answer requests made by her on behalf of true lovers, and her third wish was not to wish to be married again. Having been granted all these wishes, Dwynwen devoted her life to serving God. The remains of her church are to be seen on the island of Llanddwyn, off Anglesey.

Gwrtheyrn

Gwrtheyrn *(Vortigern)* who lived around 400 AD is seen as the traitorous British King who allowed the Saxons to settle in Kent. He was forced to flee, and settled at Nant Gwrtheyrn on the northern coast of Arfon, where the Welsh Language and Culture Centre is situated today. As punishment, monks had sworn that his death would not be a natural one and it is said that he was either killed by lightning or was forced to jump to death from a rock overlooking the sea, still called Carreg y Llam *(Leap Stone)*. Another version suggests that he spent the remainder of his days as a wanderer.

Gelert

Gelert was the dog of Llywelyn Fawr (Llywelyn the Great, who died in 1240). After returning home from a hunt, Llywelyn saw Gelert dripping with blood and his son's cradle overturned. Llywelyn jumped to the conclusion that Gelert had killed his son, and he immediately slew the dog, only to find a wolf's body beside his son who was still alive. This is a Welsh version of a folk tale that has been recounted in most European languages. In an attempt to justify the place name Beddgelert, David Pritchard, from South Wales, who became landlord of the Royal Goat Hotel at Beddgelert in 1800, erected a grave in a field and attributed it to Llywelyn's dog. Visitors to Beddgelert have taken to this story ('bedd' means 'grave', so Beddgelert = *The Grave of Gelert*) but Gelert was probably an Irish saint or a Celtic warrior of the 6th century.

The Holy Grail

A wooden bowl had been carefully kept by the family of Nanteos, a mansion not far from Aberystwyth. There is a belief that this was the cup used by Christ at the Last Supper, and that this was the Holy Grail which was sought by King Arthur's knights. It had been brought to Glastonbury by Joseph of Arimathea, and it was then taken to Strata Florida Abbey in West Wales. It is said that it had great healing powers. It is now kept in Herefordshire, in the possession of the Powell family who left Nanteos in the 1960s.

Cantre'r Gwaelod
(*The lowland hundred/settlement*)

The 13th century manuscript, *Llyfr Du Caerfyrddin* (The Black Book of Carmarthen) relates how Cardigan Bay was submerged. The earliest version suggests that the land was drowned when Mererid, a well-maiden, ignored her duties. A later version says that the land was defended by a large dyke, under the care of Seithennin. One evening he became drunk and forgot to close the sluices. As a result, the sea rushed in and drowned the inhabitants. It is said that the church bells of Cantre'r Gwaelod can be heard on still days.

Twm Siôn Cati

Although Twm Siôn Cati (1530-1609) was probably a respectable gentleman and poet, many tales have become attached to him, suggesting he was a Robin Hood figure. One story describes how he disguised himself as a poor farmer, riding an old horse. His saddle bags were full of shells, as he knew that a highwayman was about to ambush him. When accosted by the highwayman, Twm threw the bags over the hedge and the highwayman jumped over to retrieve them. In the meantime Twm leapt onto the robber's horse, and rode away with money that had already been stolen.

Lady of the Lake

Llyn y Fan Fach is a lake on the northern side of the Carmarthen Beacons. The son of a local farmer fell in love with a lady who appeared from the lake. After his third attempt to offer her bread, she promised to marry him on condition that he would not hit her three times without cause. Her dowry included the best stock of animals in the country. She was once reluctant to attend a baptism; on another occassion she wept at a wedding and then laughed at a funeral. On each of these occasions she was lightly struck by her husband and following the third blow she returned to the lake with her animals. Her three sons became famous as the 'Physicians of Myddfai' due to the folk remedies they had been taught by their mother. These remedies were recorded in 13th century manuscripts.

Arthur

Many stories have been told of King Arthur in most parts of the country. The one concerning a Welsh drover is associated with Craig y Dinas, in the Vale of Neath. The man concerned met a wizard in London who wanted to know from which tree he had cut his stick. At the base of the tree they found a cave where King Arthur and his warriors were sleeping beside heaps of gold and silver. The wizard told the drover that he could take the gold and silver as long as he did not ring a bell which was at the entrance. He did this accidentally twice, but when the warriors asked him whether it was day, he remembered to tell them to sleep on. The third time, however, he failed to reply and was badly beaten by the warriors.

This is a Welsh version of a popular international folk tale on the theme of the vanished hero who does not die. Welsh poets prophesied the return of a Welsh hero to lead the country in its hour of need, and such heroes have included Arthur and Glyndŵr as well as Cynan, Cadwaladr and Owain.

The final result of the vote on a National Assembly for Wales is declared in Cardiff (photograph: Keith Morris)

government in wales

The National Assembly for Wales

The enthusiasm of Ron Davies, the Labour Secretary of State for Wales, for establishing a National Assembly for Wales, helped by only a few other Labour MPs, but with the support of the 4 Plaid Cymru MPs and the 2 Welsh Liberal-Democrats, was instrumental in gaining a narrow victory in the 1997 referendum. Set up in 1999, the Assembly is responsible for decision making in the fields which were previously in the hands of the Welsh Office. The Secretary of State for Wales, a London Government appointed minister, had previously ruled over the Welsh Office in a quasi-colonialist manner. With the Assembly, democratic control of internal affairs was ensured, although at first the Assembly will have no tax-raising or law-making powers of its own. The Assembly will have 60 members, 40 of whom representing individual constituenices, and 20 earning their place through a system of proportional representaion.

Local Government

Wales is now divided into 22 unitary local authorities, each of which is responsible for the whole range of local authority services in its area. These include education, housing, social services, leisure, roads, town planning and other fields.

Many Welsh entertainers have become famous across the world. These include actors Richard Burton (1925-1984), Anthony Hopkins (1937-), Kenneth Griffith (1921-), Ruth Madoc (1943-) and Siân Phillips (1934-). Opera singers include Geraint Evans (1922-1992), Bryn Terfel (1963-), Gwyneth Jones (1936-) and Rebecca Evans (1964-). Among the popular entertainers and singers are Ivor Novello (1893-1951), Shirley Bassey (1937-), Max Boyce (1943-), Tommy Cooper (1922-1984), Mary Hopkin (1950-), Tom Jones (1940-), Harry Secombe (1921-) and Bonnie Tyler (1953-).

There has been a revival in popular culture, and many Welsh language singers and groups are well known to a Welsh audience. (Recently many rock groups are performing bilingually, and these are attracting attention in England and in many other countries. They include Mike Peters and his group, The Alarm, Catatonia, Gorky's Zygotic Mynci and the Super Furry Animals.)

Welsh language singers include Dafydd Iwan, a folk singer who runs the large record company Sain. Other popular names include Caryl Parry Jones, a talented singer and song writer, and Bryn Fôn, a singer and actor.

Television exposure, the setting up of several record companies, the regular playing of CDs and cassettes on Welsh radio, and Welsh gigs have contributed to this growing scene. The two national Eisteddfodau also have tents where Welsh rock groups are to be heard, and Gŵyl y Cnapan, in Ffostrasol, Ceredigion, held in July, has developed into a national rock festival.

Another popular rock festival is held at Dolgellau, and Welsh groups perform regularly in Clwb Ifor Bach, Cardiff, Y Cŵps, Aberystwyth and in many other venues.

Cerys from the group Catatonia

the future for wales

At the beginning of the third millennium, it seems that a national future for Wales is assured. Wales is likely to gain a separate political existence, and its cultural and economic life will be arranged on national lines. It remains to be seen what kind of Welshness will survive. It could develop along Irish lines, where the Irish language does not seem central to national identity, though it is still important for many Irish people. Since Wales is so closely linked to England, both geographically and economically, the Welsh language is seen by many to be the main distinguishing characteristic and the survival of Welsh will eventually be the key to the survival of Wales as a nation.

The Welsh language has received a considerable boost during the second half of the twentieth century. It is now used more than ever in education and broadcasting, and as an official language. A cause of concern, however, is how much Welsh will be used in homes and in society at large. Welsh must be used as the main language of communication in Welsh-

"Wales is not for Sale" – a slogan painted in Elan Valley

Slot Meithrin, *creating a new interest in the Welsh language in the younger generation (photograph courtesy of S4C)*

speaking Wales and increasingly used in English-speaking Wales.

It is the use of Welsh as the natural language of people and society that will eventually decide its fate, and the fate of Wales. Parents, and the new generation of young Welsh speakers, have to shoulder this responsibility, and the government must provide adequate resources for Welsh to be widely taught, used and developed.

a taste of welsh

Pronunciation Guide

Welsh is much easier to pronounce than English, as most letters have just one sound. Almost all consonants have one sound, while some vowels vary slightly. Welsh has seven vowel letters: a, e, i, o, u, w, y. The stress on Welsh words is almost always on the last syllable but one.

The Welsh Alphabet

	English sound	Welsh example	Rough pronunciation	Meaning
a	a (short, e.g. gala)	dant	dant	*tooth*
	ah (long, e.g. park)	tân	tahn	*fire*
b	b	baban	bahban	*baby*
c	k	ci	kee	*dog*
ch	ch (e.g. 'loch')	bach	Bach (composer)	*small*
d	d	dyn	deen	*man*
dd	th (voiced, e.g. that)	dydd	deeth	*day*
e	e (short, e.g. went)	pert	pehrt	*pretty*
	eh (long, e.g. café)	peth	pehth	*thing*
	ee (after 'a' and 'o', e.g. week)	mae	mahee	*there is*
		oes?	oys	*is there?*
f	v	fe	veh	*him*
ff	ff (e.g. off)	fferm	ffehrm	*farm*
g	g (hard e.g. game)	gardd	gahrth	*garden*
ng	usually ng (e.g. wing)	angen	ahngehn	*need*
	n-g (e.g. angry)	Bangor	Ban-gor	*Bangor*
h	h	hi	hee	*she*
i	i (short, as in pin)	pin	pin	*pin*
	ee (long, as in week)	sgrîn	sgreen	*screen*

j	j	jam	jam	*jam*
l	l	lôn	loan	*lane*
ll	ll (as 'l', but blow voicelessly)	lle	lleh	*place*
m	m	mam	mam	*mum*
n	n	ni	nee	*we*
o	o (short, as in **g**o**n**e)	ton	tohn	*wave*
	oa (long, as in **fore**)	côr	coar	*choir*
p	p	plant	plant	*children*
ph	ff	traphont	traffont	*viaduct*
r	r (trilled)	radio	rahdyo	*radio*
rh	rh (trilled with h)	rhaff	rhahff	*rope*
s	s (as in **s**oon)	sut?	sit?	*how?*
t	t	tŷ	tee	*house*
th	th (voiceless, as in **th**ing)	cath	kahth	*cat*
u	i (short, as in p**i**n)	punt	pihnt	*pint*
	usually ee (long, as in w**ee**k)	un	een	*one*
	(In north Wales, 'u' is pronounced like the French 'u')	pur	'pur'	*pure*
w	oo (short as in p**u**ll)	hwn	hoon	*this*
	oo (long, as in f**oo**l)	cŵn	koon	*dogs*
y	i (short, as in p**i**n)	hyn	hin	*these*
	uh (as in f**u**n) usually at the start of words	gyrru	guhree	*to drive*
	ee (long, as in w**ee**k) usually at the end of words	prynu	pruhnee	*to buy*

Other combinations

si	sh	siop	shop	*shop*
wy	ooee	rwy	rooee	*I am*
sh	sh	brwsh	broosh	*brush*

If you see a '^' accent on the last syllable of a word, the accent is on the last syllable.

Many Welsh words in recent times have been borrowed from English, and are pronounced similarly to the English words, although the spelling can be a little different. Here are some common words which sound similar to English words and which mean the same.

Welsh	English
bag	*bag*
banc	*bank*
beic	*bike*
bet	*bet*
camel	*camel*
camera	*camera*
car	*car*
casét	*cassette*
cês	*case*
cic	*kick*
clip	*clip*
cloc	*clock*
coffi	*coffee*
desg	*desk*
eliffant	*elephant*
fideo	*video*
fforc	*fork*
ffresh	*fresh*
gêm	*game*
gôl	*goal*
golff	*golf*
inc	*ink*
jam	*jam*
jîns	*jeans*
lamp	*lamp*
lifft	*lift*
lili	*lilly*
map	*map*
marmalêd	*marmalade*
mat	*mat*
nonsens	*nonsense*
pac	*pack*
parc	*park*
pas	*pass*
pensil	*pencil*
pin	*pin*
pinc	*pink*
pot	*pot*
problem	*problem*
record	*record*
reis	*rice*

sgrîn	screen
sinema	cinema
soser	saucer
tacsi	taxi
tap	tap
tic	tick
toffi	toffee
tomato	tomato
tun	tin
tywel	towel
wats	watch
winc	wink

peint	peheent	pint
plwg	ploog	plug
radio	rahdyo	radio
sgwâr	sgooahr	square
siec	sheck	cheque
sosban	sauceban	saucepan
stryd	streed	street
tâp	tahp	tape
traffig	traffig	traffic
trên	trehn	train
theatr	thehatr	theatre

Other words in Welsh are fairly similar to English and are readily understood although they have changed a little more:

Welsh	pronunciation	English
albwm	alboom	album
basged	bahsged	basket
bws	boos	bus
carped	kahrped	carpet
coleg	koleg	college
cot	cot	coat
ffrâm	ffrahm	frame
ffws	ffoos	fuss
oren	ohrehn	orange
palas	pahlahs	palace
papur	pahpir	paper

Welsh Sentences

Sentences in Welsh begin with the verb. This is followed by the subject (the 'doer' of the sentence).

All verbs in Welsh senctences can be in two parts:

1. The verb 'to be', which gives the 'time' and 'person' of the following verb
2. The main sentence verb.

The subject is put between these two, and the second verb is linked by a joining word ''n' (after vowels) or 'yn':

The object is then put after the second verb.

VERB 'TO BE'	SUBJECT	VERB	REST OF SENTENCE
e.g.			
Mae	Sian	yn prynu	record
	Sian	*is buying a*	*record*

To form the past tense ('have' or 'has' in English), simply replace 'yn' by 'wedi':

e.g.

Mae	Sian	wedi prynu	record
	Sian	*has bought a*	*record*

PRESENT TENSE

Bod (*to be*)

rwy *or* wi	*I am*
rwyt ti	*you are*
mae e	*he / it is*
mae hi	*she / it is*
mae Huw	*Huw is*
mae'r plant	*the children are*
ry'n ni	*we are*
ry'ch chi	*you are*
maen nhw	*they are*

(**NOTE:** The form 'ti' (*you*) is used with friends, the family and animals. It corresponds to the English 'thou'. 'Chi'(*you*) is used for people you don't know so well, and for the plural meaning of *you*.)

In sentences:

verb 'to be'	subject	verb	object	meaning
rwy	(fi)	'n codi		*I'm getting up*
rwyt	ti	'n gyrru	car	*you're driving a car*
mae	e	'n dod		*he's coming*
mae	hi	'n mynd		*she's going*
mae	Huw	'n bwyta	cinio	*Huw is eating lunch*
ry'n	ni	'n yfed	cwrw	*we're drinking beer*
ry'ch	chi	'n aros		*you're waiting*
ry'n	ni	'n prynu	record	*we're buying a record*
maen	nhw	'n gwerthu	cardiau	*they're selling cards*

Question forms:

ydw i?	*am I?*
wyt ti?	*are you?*
ydy e?	*is he /it?*
ydy hi?	*is she / it?*
ydy Huw?	*is Huw?*
ydy'r plant?	*are the children?*
ydyn ni?	*are we?*
ydych chi?	*are you?*
ydyn nhw?	*are they?*

Answers:

Yes: *No* – na

ydw (*I am*)
wyt (*you are*)
ydy (*he/it is*)
ydy (*she/it is*)
ydy (*Huw is*)
ydyn (*they are*)
ydyn (*we are*)
ydych (*you are*)
ydyn (*they are*)

In questions:

verb 'to be'	subject	verb	object	meaning
ydw	i	'n dal	bws?	*Am I catching a bus?*
wyt	ti	'n hoffi	coffi?	*Do you like coffee?*
ydy	e	'n gallu	nofio?	*Is he able to swim?*
ydy	hi	'n yfed	jin?	*Is she drinking gin?*
ydy	Huw	'n yfed	cwrw?	*Is Huw drinking beer?*
ydy	'r plant	yn yfed	pop?	*Are the children drinking pop?*
ydyn	ni	'n hoffi	disgos?	*Do we like discos?*
ydyn	nhw	'n prynu	tocyn?	*Are they buying a ticket?*

Notice that the question can either mean *'am I'* or *'do I'* etc.

Negative forms:

		Other forms sometimes heard
dw i ddim	*I am not*	Dydw i ddim
dwyt ti ddim	*you are not*	
dyw e ddim	*he / it is not*	Dydy o ddim
dyw hi ddim	*she / it is not*	Dydy hi ddim
dyw Huw ddim	*Huw is not*	Dydy Huw ddim
dyw'r plant ddim	*the children are not*	Dydy'r plant ddim
dy'n ni ddim	*we are not*	Dydyn ni ddim
dy'ch chi ddim	*you are not*	Dydych chi ddim
dy'n nhw ddim	*they are not*	Dydyn nhw ddim

In sentences:

verb 'to be'	sub-ject	ddim (*not*)	verb	object	meaning
Dw	i	ddim	yn prynu	record	*I'm not buying a record*
Dwyt	ti	ddim	yn chwarae	rygbi	*You're not playing rugby*
Dyw	e	ddim	yn dal	bws	*He isn't catching a bus*
Dyw	hi	ddim	yn dal	trên	*She isn't catching a train*
Dyw	Huw	ddim	yn yfed	cwrw	*Huw isn't drinking beer*
Dyw	'r plant	ddim	yn bwyta	tomatos	*The children aren't eating tomatoes*
Dy'n	ni	ddim	yn bwyta	reis	*We're not eating rice*
Dy'ch	chi	ddim	yn hoffi	coffi	*You don't like coffee*
Dy'n	nhw	ddim	yn hoffi	toffi	*You don't like toffee*

PAST TENSE '*HAS*' AND '*HAVE*':

The same as the present tense, but replace 'yn' by 'wedi'
In sentences:

verb 'to be'	subject	verb	object	meaning
rwy	(fi)	wedi codi		*I have got up*
rwyt	ti	wedi gyrru	car	*you have driven a car*
mae	e	wedi dod		*he has come*
mae	hi	wedi mynd		*she has gone*
mae	Huw	wedi bwyta	cinio	*Huw has eaten lunch*
mae	'r plant	wedi yfed	pop	*The children have drunk pop*
ry'n	ni	wedi yfed	cwrw	*we have drunk beer*
ry'ch	chi	wedi aros		*you have waited*
maen	nhw	wedi gwerthu	cardiau	*they have sold cards*

Some Common Verbs

aros	*wait, stay*
bwyta	*eat*
cael	*have*
caru	*love*
cerdded	*walk*
codi	*get up*
cwrdd â	*meet*
cysgu	*sleep*
dal	*catch*
darllen	*read*
dechrau	*begin*
dod	*come*
edrych ar	*look at*
eistedd	*sit*
gallu	*can, be able to*
golchi	*wash*
gorffen	*end*
gweld	*see*
gwerthu	*buy*
gwneud	*do*
gyrru	*drive*
hoffi	*like*
moyn	*want to*
mynd	*go*
prynu	*sell*
rhedeg	*run*
sefyll	*stand*
teithio	*travel*
yfed	*drink*
ysgrifennu	*write*

Some Common Nouns

y bachgen	*the boy*
bara	*bread*
y bobl	*the people*
bwrdd	*table*
canolfan siopa	*shopping centre*
y car	*the car*
cerdyn post	*post card*
cig	*meat*
coffi	*coffee*
cwpan	*cup*
cwrw	*beer*
y dafarn	*the pub*
y ddinas	*the city*
ydref	*the town*
y dyn	*the man*
y fenyw	*the woman*
y ferch	*the girl*
fforc	*fork*
ffrwythau	*fruit*
y gadair	*the chair*
y ganolfan hamdden	*the leisure centre*
y garej	*the garage*
gwin	*wine*

y gyllell	knife
llaeth	milk
llawr	floor
llety	accommodation
llwy	spoon
llyfr	book
llysiau	vegetables
neuadd y dref	the town hall
papur	paper
y plant	the children
plât	plate
pwll nofio	swimming pool
y sinema	the cinema
y siop	the shop
y stafell	the room
y stamp	stamp
y stryd	the street
te	tea
y tŷ bach	the toilet
y tŷ	the house
y wlad	the country

Days of the Week

dydd Llun	Monday
dydd Mawrth	Tuesday
dydd Mercher	Wednesday
dydd Iau	Thursday
dydd Gwener	Friday
dydd Sadwrn	Saturday
dydd Sul	Sunday

Months of the Year

Ionawr	January
Chwefror	February
Mawrth	March
Ebrill	April
Mai	May
Mehefin	June
Gorffennaf	July
Awst	August
Medi	September
Hydref	October
Tachwedd	November
Rhagfyr	December

Place Names

Aberdâr	Aberdare
Aberdaugleddau	Milford Haven
Aberhonddu	Brecon
Abermo	Barmouth
Abertawe	Swansea
Aberteifi	Cardigan
Bae Colwyn	Colwyn Bay
Bryste	Bristol
Caerdydd	Cardiff
Caerffili	Caerphilly

Caergybi	*Holyhead*
Casllwchwr	*Loughor*
Casnewydd	*Newport*
Castell-nedd	*Neath*
Dinbych	*Denbigh*
Dinbych y Pysgod	*Tenby*
Dulyn	*Dublin*
Hendy-gwyn	*Whitland*
Lerpwl	*Liverpool*
Llundain	*London*
Merthyr Tudful	*Merthyr Tydfil*
Morgannwg	*Glamorgan*
Pen-y-bont	*Bridgend*
Penfro	*Pembroke*
Rhufain	*Rome*
Rhydychen	*Oxford*
Talyllychau	*Talley*
Trefdraeth	*Newport (Pemb.)*
Tyddewi	*St David's*
Wrecsam	*Wrexham*
Y Barri	*Barry*
Y Fenni	*Abergavenny*
Y Trallwng	*Welshpool*

Questions

What?	**Beth?**
What's your name?	Beth yw'ch enw chi?
What is ... in Welsh?	Beth yw ... yn Gymraeg?
What's the price of the ... ?	Beth yw pris y ... ?
What's the price of the record?	Beth yw pris y record?
Where?	**Ble?**
Where is ... ?	Ble mae ... ?
Where is the station?	Ble mae'r orsaf?
Where do you live?	Ble ry'ch chi'n byw?
From where do you come?	O ble ry'ch chi'n dod?
	Un o ble y'ch chi?
When?	**Pryd?**
When does the train leave?	Pryd mae'r trên yn gadael?
When does the film start?	Pryd mae'r ffilm yn dechrau?
When does the bus arrive?	Pryd mae'r bws yn cyrraedd?
How much?	**Faint?**
How much is it?	Faint yw e?
How much are they?	Faint y'n nhw?
May I... / May I have...?	**Ga i?**
May I have a peint?	Ga i beint?
May I help?	Ga i helpu?
Who?	**Pwy?**
Who is coming?	Pwy sy'n dod?
Who are you?	Pwy ydych chi?
Who is there?	Pwy sy 'na?
Have you got ... ?	Oes ... 'da chi?
Have you got a car?	Oes car 'da chi?
Have you got a ticket?	Oes tocyn 'da chi?
How?	**Sut? Shwd?**
How are you?	Sut da'ch chi? (*in N. Wales*)
	Shwd y'ch chi? (*in S. Wales*)

Why?	**Pam?**
Why is he coming?	Pam mae e'n dod?
Why are we going?	Pam ydyn ni'n mynd?

Greetings

Hello	Helo
Hi!	Shwmae (*South Wales*)
	S'mae (*North Wales*)
How are you?	Shwd ych chi (*South Wales*)
	Sut 'dach chi (*North Wales*)
Good morning	Bore da
Good afternoon	Prynhawn da
Good evening	Noswaith dda
Good night	Nos da
Good bye	Pob hwyl; hwyl; da boch chi
Good health!	Iechyd da!
Come in	Dewch i mewn
Happy birthday!	Pen blwydd hapus!
Merry Christmas!	Nadolig Llawen!
Pleased to meet you	Falch i gwrdd â chi
I'm John	John ydw i
This is Jane	Dyma Jane
All the best!	Pob hwyl!
Welcome	Croeso
Sit down	Eisteddwch
Excuse me	Esgusodwch fi
It's fine	Mae hi'n braf
Speak slowly	Siaradwch yn araf

Once again	Unwaith eto
I'm learning Welsh	Rwy'n dysgu Cymraeg
Replies	
Very well thanks	Da iawn diolch
Fine thanks	Iawn diolch
All right	Gweddol
Thank you very much	Diolch yn fawr iawn
Thank you	Diolch yn fawr
Thanks	Diolch
Welcome!	Croeso!

Useful Phrases

WHERE IS...?	
Where's the station?	Ble mae'r orsaf?
library?	llyfrgell?
bus station?	orsaf bysiau?
house?	tŷ?
theatre?	theatr?
cinema?	sinema?
college?	coleg?
market?	farchnad?
shop?	siop?
park?	parc?
river?	afon?
street?	stryd?
square?	sgwâr?
bank?	banc?

Drinks

a pint of bitter	peint o chwerw
a pint of lager	peint o lager
a pint of Guinness	peint o Guinness
half a pint	hanner peint
half a pint of beer	hanner peint o gwrw
two pints	dau beint
two pints of beer	dau beint o gwrw
three pints	tri pheint
three pints of beer	tri pheint o gwrw
one red wine	un gwin coch
one white wine	un gwin gwyn
one dry white wine	un gwin gwyn sych
one sweet white wine	un gwin gwyn melys
two red wines	dau win coch
two white wines	dau win gwyn
one pint of beer	un peint o gwrw
and one white wine	ac un gwin gwyn
orange juice	sudd oren
apple juice	sudd afal
a bottle of wine	potel o win
water	dŵr
with ice	gyda iâ
do you want ice?	ydych chi'n moyn iâ?
	ydych chi eisiau iâ?

The Weather

It's fine today	Mae hi'n braf heddiw
It's raining	Mae hi'n bwrw glaw
It's dry	Mae hi'n sych
It's cloudy	Mae hi'n gymylog
It's cold	Mae hi'n oer
It's wet	Mae hi'n wlyb
Is it raining?	Ydy hi'n bwrw glaw?
Yes	Ydy
No	Na
Is it snowing?	Ydy hi'n bwrw eira?
Is it sunny?	Ydy hi'n heulog?
Will it be fine tomorrow?	Fydd hi'n braf yfory?
Yes	Bydd
No	Na
Will it rain tomorrow?	Fydd hi'n bwrw glaw yfory?
How's the weather now?	Sut mae'r tywydd nawr?

I've got ...

I've got a car	Mae car 'da fi
Have you got a car?	Oes car 'da chi?
Yes	Oes
No	Na
Have you got a film?	Oes ffilm 'da chi?
I've got a camera	Mae camera 'da fi
Have you got a bath?	Oes bath 'da chi?

Staying the Night

Have you got room?	Oes lle 'da chi?
... for one, for two, for three	... i un, i ddau, i dri
What is the cost?	Beth yw'r gost?
Is there a reduction for children?	Oes gostyngiad i blant?
How long are you staying?	Am faint ydych chi'n aros?
I'm staying for two nights	Rwy'n aros am ddwy noson
Is there a T.V. in the room?	Oes teledu yn y stafell?
Yes	Oes
When can I pay?	Pryd galla i dalu?
Where is the kitchen?	Ble mae'r gegin?
Where is the toilet?	Ble mae'r tŷ bach?
From where do you come?	Un o ble ydych chi?
I come from Cardiff	Rwy'n dod o Gaerdydd
Where is the nearest pub?	Ble mae'r dafarn agosa?

Buying Tickets

I want two tickets	Rwy'n moyn dau docyn
One adult, one child	Un oedolyn, un plentyn
please	os gwelwch yn dda
One ticket to Swansea	Un tocyn i Abertawe
ticket office	swyddfa docynnau
left luggage	stafell fagiau
When does the train leave?	Pryd mae'r trên yn gadael?
When does the bus leave?	Pryd mae'r bws yn gadael?
From which platform?	O ba blatfform?
Where's the bus stop?	Ble mae'r arhosfan?
Is the bus due?	Ydy'r bws ar ddod?

Is the train late?	Ydy'r trên yn hwyr?
Yes, as usual	Ydy, fel arfer
Is the train punctual?	Ydy'r trên yn brydlon?
No	Na
Thanks	Diolch

Buying Gifts

What do you want?	Beth ydych chi'n moyn?
Have you got gifts?	Oes anrhegion 'da chi?
Have you got pottery?	Oes crochenwaith 'da chi?
Yes	Oes
Do you sell calendars?	Ydych chi'n gwerthu calendrau?
Do you sell postcards?	Ydych chi'n gwerthu cardiau post?
Have you got books for learners?	Oes llyfrau i ddysgwyr 'da chi?
Have you got Welcome to Welsh?	Ydy Welcome to Welsh 'da chi?
Yes	Ydy
How much is the cassette?	Faint yw'r casét?
I'm looking for a dictionary	Rwy'n chwilio am eiriadur

Numbers

1	un
2	dau
3	tri or tair
4	pedwar or pedair
5	pump or pum
6	chwech or chwe
7	saith
8	wyth

9	naw	castell	castle
10	deg	cefn	back, ridge
11	un deg un	coed	trees
12	un deg dau *or* deuddeg	cwm	valley
13	un deg tri	dinas	city
14	un deg pedwar	du	black
15	un deg pump	eglwys	church
16	un deg chwech	gelli	grove
17	un deg saith	glan	bank
18	un deg wyth *or* deunaw	glyn	vale
19	un deg naw	hir	long
20	dau ddeg *or* ugain	isaf	lower
30	tri deg	llan	church
40	pedwar deg	llyn	lake
50	pum deg *or* hanner cant	maen	stone
100	cant	maes	field
1000	mil	melin	mill
		mynydd	mountain

Meanings of Place Names

Welsh place names often describe the location of the geographical position of the place. Here are the meanings of some of the elements that make up Welsh place names:

aber	*mouth of river*	nant	*brook*
blaen	*head of valley*	newydd	*new*
bryn	*hill*	pen	*head, top*
cae	*field*	plas	*mansion*
caer	*fort*	pont	*bridge*
		rhaeadr	*waterfall*
		tref	*town, house*
		uchaf	*upper*
		y	*the, of the*

The National Anthem

The Welsh national anthem was written by Evan James and his son James in Pontypridd in 1856, and was first performed in Maesteg. It won a prize at the national eisteddfod at Llangollen in 1858 and by 1866 it was recognized as the national anthem.

Hen Wlad fy Nhadau

Mae hen wlad fy nhadau yn annwyl i mi,
Gwlad beirdd a chantorion enwogion o fri;
Ei gwrol ryfelwyr, gwladgarwyr tra mad,
Dros ryddid collasant eu gwaed.

Chorus:
Gwlad, gwlad,
Pleidiol wyf i'm gwlad;
Tra môr yn fur i'r bur hoff bau,
O bydded i'r heniaith barhau.

Land of my Fathers

The land of my fathers, the land of my choice,
The land in which poets and minstrels rejoice;
The land whose stern warriors were true to the core,
While bleeding for freedom of yore.

Chorus:
Wales! Wales!
Fav'rite land of Wales!
While see he wall, may naught befall
To mar the old language of Wales.

information contacts

The international dialling code for Wales is 44. Dial your international access code (e.g. 00), followed by 44, followed by the telephone number omitting the initial 0.

National Museum of Wales
Cathays Park, Cardiff CF1 3NP
☎01222 397951 🖷373219
🖳http://www.cardiff.ac.uk/nmgw/locate.html

Museum of Welsh Life
Sain Ffagan, Cardiff CF5 6XB ☎01222 569441
🖳http://www.cardiff.ac.uk/nmgw/stfagans.html

BBC Cymru/Wales
Llandaf, Cardiff, CF5 2YQ ☎01222 572888
🖳http://www.bbc.co.uk/wales/

Welsh Language Board
5-7 St Mary's Street, Cardiff, CF1 2AT
☎01222 224744 🖷224577 🖷bwrdd_yr_iaith@netwales.co.uk
🖳http://www.netwales.co.uk/byig

Books Council of Wales
Castell Brychan, Aberystwyth, Ceredigion SY23 2JB
☎01970 624151 🖷625385 🖷castellbrychan@cllc.org.uk
🖳http://www.wbc.org.uk

National Library of Wales
Aberystwyth, Ceredigion SY23 3BU
☎01970 632800 🖷615709 🖳http://www.nlw.org.uk

S4C
Parc Tŷ Glas, Llanisien, Cardiff CF4 5DU
☎01222 747444 🖷754444 🖳http://www.s4c.co.uk

National Eisteddfod of Wales
40 Parc Tŷ Glas, Llanisien, Cardiff CF4 5WU
☎01222 763777 🖷237071 🖳http://www.eisteddfod.org.uk

University of Wales
Cathays Park, Cardiff ☎01222 382656

Welsh Arts Council
9 Museum Street, Cardiff ☎01222 394711

Cadw (Welsh Heritage)
Brunel House, 2 Fitzalan Road, Cardiff CF2 1UY
☎01222 500200 🖷500300

Wales Tourist Board
Brunel House, 2 Fitzalan Road, Cardiff CF2 1UY
☎01222 499909 🖳http://www.tourism.wales.gov.uk

Welsh Joint Education Committee
245 Western Avenue, Cardiff CF5 2YX ☎01222 265007
⌨http://www.wjec.co.uk ✉info@wjec.co.uk

Glamorgan County Cricket Club
Sophia Gardens, Cardiff ☎01222 343478

Cymdeithas yr Iaith (Welsh Language Society)
15 Rhodfa'r Gogledd, Aberystwyth, Ceredigion SY23 2JH
☎01970 624501 ▤627122 ✉swyddfa@cymdeithas.com

Welsh Sports Council
Sophia Gardens, Cardiff ☎01222 397571

CYD (Learners Association)
Yr Hen Goleg, Aberyswyth ☎01970 622143

Mudiad Ysgolion Meithrin (Welsh Playgroup Movement)
145 Albany Road, Roath, Cardiff ☎01222 485510

Plaid Cymru
18 Park Grove, Caerdydd CF1 3BN ☎01222 646000 ▤646001
✉post@plaidcymru.org ⌨http://www.plaidcymru.org

Urdd Gobaith Cymru (Welsh League of Youth)
Ffordd Llanbadarn, Aberystwyth, Ceredigion SY23 1EU
☎01970 623744 ▤626120 ✉urdd@urdd.demon.co.uk
⌨http://www.urdd.org

Books

For Welsh books and books on Welsh interests, visit a local Welsh bookshop (there is one in most towns) or write to the Books Council of Wales. Welsh books are now available also at WH Smiths, Waterstones and other booksellers. Y Lolfa (publishers of this book) have an attractive web site at www.ylolfa.com

CDs, Cassettes & Videos

These are mainly available at Welsh bookshops. They can also be obtained from the recording companies, such as Sain, Llandwrog, Caernarfon, Gwynedd LL54 5TG
☎01286 831111 ▤831497 ✉music@sain.wales.com
⌨http://www.sain.wales.com

Learning Welsh

Contact the Welsh for Adults Tutor at The University of Wales Bangor, Aberystwyth, Swansea and Cardiff, or any local authority. A list of courses can be obtained from the Welsh for Adults Officer, Welsh Language Board, 5-7 St Mary's Street, Cardiff, CF1 2AT (01222 224774).

Tourism

Contact any local authority, or the Welsh Tourist Board at Brunel House, 2 Fitzalan Road, Cardiff CF2 1UY (01222 499909).

further reading

Aitchison, J and Carter, H, *A Geography of the Welsh Language*, University of Wales Press, 1994.

Andrews, J A and Henshaw, L G, *The Welsh Language and the Courts*, University of Wales Aberystwyth, 1984.

Betts, Clive, *Culture in Crisis*, The Ffynnon Press, Merseyside, 1976.

Bromwich, Rachel, *Dafydd ap Gwilym, a selection of poems*, Penguin Books, 1985.

Clancy, Joseph P, *The Earliest Welsh Poetry*, Macmillan, 1970.

Clancy, Joseph P, *Medieval Welsh Lyrics*, Macmillan, 1965.

Davies, Janet, *The Welsh Language*, University of Wales Press, 1993.

Davies, John, *A History of Wales*, Penguin, 1993.

Davies, John, *Broadcasting and the BBC in Wales*, University of Wales Press, Cardiff, 1994.

Davies, R R, *The Age of Conquest*, Oxford University Press, 1991.

Davies, R R, *The Revolt of Owain Glyndŵr*, Oxford University Press, 1995.

Evans, D Gareth, *A History of Wales 1815-1906*, University of Wales Press, 1989.

Evans, Gwynfor, *A National Future for Wales*, Plaid Cymru, 1975.

Gwyndaf, Robin, *Welsh Folk Tales*, National Museum of Wales, Cardiff, 1989.

Henken, Elissa R, *National Redeemer, Owain Glyndŵr in Welsh Tradition*, University of Wales Press, 1996.

Hume I, and Pryce, W (eds.), *The Welsh and Their Country*, 1986.

Jenkins, Geraint H, *The Foundations of Modern Wales*, Oxford University Press, 1993.

Johnston, Dafydd, *The Literature of Wales*, University of Wales Press, 1994.

Jones, Graham, *The History of Wales*, University of Wales Press, 1990

May, John, *Reference Wales*, University of Wales Press, 1994.

Morgan, K O, *Rebirth of a Nation, Wales 1880-1980*, Oxford University and Wales University Press, 1982.

Morgan, P and Thomas, D, *Wales: The Shaping of a Nation*, Newton Abbot, 1984.

Owen, T, *Welsh Folk Customs*, National Museum of Wales, 1974.

Parker, M and Whitfield, P, *Wales the Rough Guide*, The Rough Guides, 1994.

Philip, A B, *The Welsh Question, Nationalism in Welsh Politics 1945-1970*, University of Wales Press, Cardiff, 1975.

Rees, W, *An Historical Atlas of Wales*, Cardiff, 1951.

Stephens, M (ed.), *The Oxford Companion to the Literature of Wales*, Oxford University Press, 1986.

Stephens, M (ed.), *The Welsh Language Today*, Gomer Press, 1979.

Williams, Gwyn A, *When Was Wales?*, Penguin, 1985.

Williams, Dafydd, *The Story of Plaid Cymru*, Plaid Cymru, 1990.

Williams, David, *A History of Modern Wales*, John Murray, London, 1962.

Writers of Wales series, University of Wales Press.